গীতাঞ্জলি

Gitanjali

Tagore's Gitanjali

A New Translation
with the Bengali Originals
and the Tagore Translations

Prasenjit Gupta

PARABAAS

First published 2023; reprint edition published 2024

Rabindranath Tagore drew from several collections of his poetry in Bengali, one of which was titled *Gitanjali*, for the poems he included in the English *Gitanjali*. He selected most of the poems (53) from the Bengali *Gitanjali*; the other works represented are the collections *Gitimalya* (16), *Naibedya* (15), *Kheya* (11), *Shishu* (3), *Chaitali* (1), *Kalpana* (1), *Smaran* (1), and *Utsarga* (1) and the play *Achalayatan*, from which one song was drawn.

The frontispiece is taken from *Gitanjali* (*Song Offerings*) by Rabindranath Tagore, Bilingual Edition, published by Rabindra-Bhavana, Visva-Bharati, Santiniketan, 2nd ed., 2015. The quotation on the back cover referring to the 1912 publication of *Gitanjali* as "an event in the history of English poetry and of world poetry" is from Ezra Pound, "Tagore's Poems," *Poetry: A Magazine of Verse*, Vol. I, No. 3, December 1912, p. 92. Six of Tagore's poems appeared in this issue.

In this reprint edition, the formatting of the Bengali poems (and of the Gupta translations) has been modified to follow that in *Gitanjali* by Rabindranath Tagore, published by Visva-Bharati, Santiniketan, *Natun Sanskaran,* 25 *Baishakh* BE 1349, reprinted *Kartik* BE 1425, and different volumes of *Rabindra-Rachanaboli* (Collected Works of Rabindranath Tagore), published by Visva-Bharati, Santiniketan, BE 1426. The formatting of Tagore's translations follows that in *Gitanjali (Song Offerings)* by Rabindra Nath Tagore, published by the India Society, 1912; first edition re-issued in facsimile by Visva-Bharati, Santiniketan, 2018.

Published by PARABAAS
12 Jason Ct, Howell, NJ 07731, USA
www.parabaas.com
parabaas@parabaas.com

Distributed in India by SUNDARBAN BOOKS
sundarbanbooks@gmail.com
+91 86091-69717

Library of Congress Control Number: 2023930051
ISBN: 978-1-946582-40-9 (hardcover)
ISBN: 978-1-946582-50-8 (paperback)

Translator's Dedication

মাকে

for my mother

Contents

Translator's Preface

When I had almost completed these translations, I mentioned the project to a couple of friends over dinner. The host, a fellow Bengali, responded immediately: "What? Gitanjali? You mean the one that Rabindranath himself translated already?—No, no, don't do that one. Pick something else. How can you improve on his own translations?"

Many Bengalis who hold Rabindranath (as most Bengalis refer to him; pronounced Ro-bin-dro-naath) far above all other Indian writers—and possibly above all other writers, above all other Indians, above all others—will no doubt react the same way. Rabindranath's place in the hearts of the people of Bengal both east and west (now Bangladesh and West Bengal respectively) is perhaps unparalleled in the English-speaking world. The songs he wrote and set to melody are still recorded frequently, mostly with their original tunes and minimal orchestration but also occasionally in unnecessarily modernized versions.

With this project, I may be similarly accused of providing an unnecessary and unsatisfying modernized version of Rabindranath's work. My friend's comments may have been a foretaste of such responses. This is my apology to those readers, if they read these poems and are disappointed with my versions. For ease of comparison, I provide each poem in the Bengali original and Rabindranath's translation, which is followed by mine. You will also note that I have sometimes taken advantage of his translations, which were the inspiration for my own and which I felt I could not, therefore, leave out of this collection.

For most Indians, *Gitanjali* is arguably still the best known modern literary work of Indian origin. It's easy to see why. It's a product of a superior mind and vision; no doubt Rabindranath stood on the shoulders of his predecessors in the Bhakti tradition—in fact he later translated a collection of Kabir's poems into English—but he brought his own singular genius to lift his work to a higher level, one that resonates strongly with many Indian readers. I have not provided an introduction to Rabindranath or his work, since an introduction that would do justice to either is not within the scope of this book. Many are widely available, in print and on the Internet, for those interested. My focus is on the poems (or songs) themselves and in trying to reproduce them in somewhat more modern renderings that are closer to the Bengali originals.

Even with that seemingly modest goal, however, I found this a very difficult task.

I use the word "translations" above to refer to Rabindranath's own prose renderings of the poems (I use "poem" and "song" interchangeably in this book; he set many of the poems to music, and they are widely available as songs), but in fact for many of these poems the translations do not hew closely to the originals; readers of Bengali will easily be able to see how they diverge. In many places Tagore combines lines to produce a compressed English version, he omits fragments and even entire lines of the Bengali, he explains the thought behind the Bengali by making the English version more explicit, and so on. Rabindranath's English versions, in other words, are versions polished to make them more accessible and appealing to readers of English poetry. His English *Gitanjali* was first published in 1912, but the poems hold up very well even now, more than a hundred years later, and often still surpass other translators' later attempts.

Here are a few examples to illustrate the changes Rabindranath made during translating these poems into English. I have also indicated a few other instances using footnotes to the relevant lines or poems.

Poem 35, which in Rabindranath's version begins "Where the mind is without fear," is perhaps the best known of his poems in English—and certainly for many Indian schoolchildren! I remember memorizing and reciting the poem in primary school, with only a hazy idea, if any, of what was meant by some of the more complex lines. (It's certainly an act of great foolishness and temerity for me to offer a revision of this classic, but his version is of course eternal.) Rabindranath renders the latter part of the poem, beginning after the comma in line 6 of the Bengali, thus:

> Where tireless striving stretches its arms towards perfection;
> Where the clear stream of reason has not lost its way into the dreary desert sand of dead habit;
> Where the mind is led forward by thee into ever-widening thought and action—
> Into that heaven of freedom, my Father, let my country awake.

My version, following the Bengali, has:

> Where the work-stream flows unrestrained,
> Runs from land to land on every side
> Towards a thousand different kinds of fulfillment—
> Where the desert sand-heaps of trivial custom
> Have not swallowed up the stream of reason
> And broken manhood a hundred ways; where always
> You are the guide in all deed and thought and joy—
> Strike hard with your own hand, oh father,
> And wake Bharat into that heaven.

Most readers might agree that "desert sand of dead habit" is much more poetic, much more powerful, than "desert sand-heaps of trivial custom," and the only excuse I can offer for not stealing Rabindranath's words (which I have unashamedly done elsewhere) is that my version follows the original slightly more closely, but other readers may differ with even that assertion.

The other changes that Rabindranath made are clear. He renders the first of these four stanzas succinctly and with immense power; my version rambles on. (Again, I follow the original closely; I have no additional excuses to offer.)

More strikingly, Rabindranath leaves out what I have translated as "broken manhood a hundred ways" and "Strike hard with your own hand," and I will not speculate why. He also translates "Bharat" as "my country," which would perhaps have been clearer to many of his readers.

At the end of poem 47, Rabindranath adds more poetry to the original by extending the image. My version has

> From looking at his compassionate face,
> My soul will tremble
>   filled with knowing him—
> Don't wake me, please, none of you,
>   it is he who will awaken me.

Rabindranath has

> The first thrill of joy to my awakened soul let it come from his glance. And let my return to myself be immediate return to him.

That last sentence—"let my return to myself be immediate return to him"—is not in the original, but it adds meaning and great elegance to the poem.

One of Rabindranath's best-known lines occurs in his version of poem 82:

> Thy centuries follow each other perfecting a small wild flower.

A line of surpassing charm and beauty, by any measure. My translation falls far short:

> Through a hundred years
> Your calm preparations continue
> To make a flower-bud bloom.

So there you have it. That's the difference between a poetic translation and a translation that stays close to the original. No comparison.

Finally, let me briefly mention two poems, numbered 61 and 102 respectively, where Rabindranath chose not to include the last two stanzas of the original in his English version. I'm not aware why he made this decision, but, as I indicate in my footnotes, for both poems I've included the entire poem in the original and in my translation.

Translators are always faced with this choice between, on the one hand, following the source text very closely, to produce what is called a literal translation, and, on the other, adopting a looser style, changing and adapting the work somewhat in the interest of producing a more readable and compelling product in the target language, one that will fit into that literature and current writing practices and tastes in reading in that language. Rabindranath himself took the latter path, as illustrated above, in his translations of these poems, and he enjoyed the further freedom, perhaps, as the writer of the source text not to feel himself constrained to offer literal renderings of his own work. He may have been translating with a specific audience in mind, that of the western readers of his work at the time. (The Irish poet W. B. Yeats wrote an enthusiastic introduction to Rabindranath's English *Gitanjali*, presenting the latter's work to the western world.)

My own approach to translation takes the first path: to offer a work that stays close to the original. I try as far as possible to translate every word of the source text and not to add anything of my own. The reasoning behind this is, of course, that if translators should add their own interpretations to the work, a dozen different translations will end up pointing a dozen different ways, and the reader of only one or two of these will never gain an accurate sense of the original. Hence the literal translation, which while lacking poetic fullness is at least as accurate a rendering—in sense if not sensibility—as the translator is able to provide. (I will not enter into a detailed discussion here of how words have multiple meanings and how even a literal translation may depart from the original, but in general the literal translator's aim is to select the meaning that seems to fit better into the sense of the line and of the poem. That is an interpretation too, certainly, but one of smaller ambition and effect.)

Literal translation sometimes results, as it undoubtedly has in my case, in lines that may sound awkward to readers of poetry in English, and that is the price I pay for seeking to stay as close to the Bengali as I can. I only hope that in trying not to hurt Rabindranath's language I have not seriously hurt his poems. Homage should not harm.

Rabindranath's songs in the original Bengali are marked by rhyme, assonance, and even some delightful wordplay that I cannot reproduce in my translations. However, I hope I have been able to convey what I believe is the spirit and grandeur of each song—the breadth of vision and the connection with a higher power, a glimpse of a guiding light, and how that connection may be experienced in the everyday world—that make Rabindranath the incomparable poet he is. You don't have to believe in God to admire these songs or to be moved by them. All you need is a sense of your own guiding spirit, and I would even say that if you don't have that sense before reading these songs, you may have it after you've read them.

This book, then, is the translator's gitanjali to the writer. I make this song-offering of my translations to Rabindranath knowing, as my friend pointed out, that I cannot improve upon his own.

গীতাঞ্জলি

Gitanjali

১ 1

আমারে তুমি অশেষ করেছ
এমনি লীলা তব।
ফুরায়ে ফেলে আবার ভরেছ
জীবন নব নব।
কত যে গিরি কত যে নদীতীরে
বেড়ালে বহি ছোটো এ বাঁশিটিরে,
কত যে তান বাজালে ফিরে ফিরে
কাহারে তাহা কব।

তোমারি ওই অমৃতপরশে
আমার হিয়াখানি
হারালো সীমা বিপুল হরষে
উথলি' উঠে বাণী।
আমার শুধু একটি মুঠি ভরি
দিতেছ দান দিবসবিভাবরী,
হল না সারা কত-না যুগ ধরি,
কেবলই আমি লব।

• • •

THOU hast made me endless, such is thy pleasure. This frail vessel thou emptiest again and again, and fillest it ever with fresh life.

This little flute of a reed thou hast carried over hills and dales, and hast breathed through it melodies eternally new.

At the immortal touch of thy hands my little heart loses its limits in joy and gives birth to utterance ineffable.

Thy infinite gifts come to me only on these very small hands of mine. Ages pass, and still thou pourest, and still there is room to fill.

• • •

You've made me endless
        That's what amuses you,
Emptied me out and filled me again
        With new life anew.
How many mountains, how many river banks
You've wandered, carrying this little flute,
How many tunes you played as you roamed—
        Whom can I tell of this.

With your immortal touch
        This my heart
Loses its bounds in enormous joy
        And words spill forth.
You give me your gifts every day, every night
And I take my tiny fistfuls—
And it never ends, age after age
        I only keep on taking.

২ 2

তুমি যখন গান গাহিতে বল
গর্ব আমার ভ'রে ওঠে বুকে;
দুই আঁখি মোর করে ছল ছল
নিমেষহারা চেয়ে তোমার মুখে।
কঠিন কটু যা আছে মোর প্রাণে
গলিতে চায় অমৃতময় গানে,
সব সাধনা আরাধনা মম
উড়িতে চায় পাখির মতো সুখে।

তৃপ্ত তুমি আমার গীতরাগে,
ভালো লাগে তোমার ভালো লাগে,
জানি আমি এই গানেরই বলে
বসি গিয়ে তোমারি সম্মুখে।
মন দিয়ে যার নাগাল নাহি পাই,
গান দিয়ে সেই চরণ ছুঁয়ে যাই,
সুরের ঘোরে আপ্‌নাকে যাই ভুলে,
বন্ধু ব'লে ডাকি মোর প্রভুকে।

◆ ◆ ◆

When thou commandest me to sing it seems that my heart would break with pride; and I look to thy face, and tears come to my eyes.

All that is harsh and dissonant in my life melts into one sweet harmony—and my adoration spreads wings like a glad bird on its flight across the sea.

I know thou takest pleasure in my singing. I know that only as a singer I come before thy presence.

I touch by the edge of the far spreading wing of my song thy feet which I could never aspire to reach.

Drunk with the joy of singing I forget myself and call thee friend who art my lord.

◆ ◆ ◆

When you tell me to sing
Pride fills up my heart;
My eyes brim over
As I stare unblinking at your face.
Whatever is hard and harsh in my life
Wants to melt away in honeyed song,
All my penitence and prayer
Wants to fly in birdlike joy.

You're content with my song and raag,
It pleases you, it does; I know
It's only on the strength of these songs
That I come and sit before you.
With my mind I cannot reach you;
With my song I touch those feet.
Drunk with melody, I forget myself—
My lord—and call you my friend.

৩ 3

তুমি কেমন করে গান কর যে, গুণী,
অবাক হয়ে শুনি কেবল শুনি।
সুরের আলো ভুবন ফেলে ছেয়ে,
সুরের হাওয়া চলে গগন বেয়ে,
পাষাণ টুটে ব্যাকুল বেগে ধেয়ে,
বহিয়া যায় সুরের সুরধুনী।

মনে করি অম্‌নি সুরে গাই,
কণ্ঠে আমার সুর খুঁজে না পাই।
কইতে কী চাই, কইতে কথা বাধে—
হার মেনে যে পরান আমার কাঁদে—
আমায় তুমি ফেলেছ কোন্ ফাঁদে
চৌদিকে মোর সুরের জাল বুনি।

• • •

I KNOW not how thou singest, my master! I ever listen in silent amazement.

The light of thy music illumines the world. The life breath of thy music runs from sky to sky. The holy stream of thy music breaks through all stony obstacles and rushes on.

My heart longs to join in thy song, but vainly struggles for a voice. I would speak, but speech breaks not into song, and I cry out baffled. Ah, thou hast made my heart captive in the endless meshes of thy music, my master!

• • •

How you sing your song, O talented one,
I listen speechless, I can only listen.

Melody's light overspreads the universe
Melody's breeze flows up from sky to sky
Breaking through boulders at its frenzied pace
It rushes on, melody's river rushes on.

In my mind I want to sing that song
But I cannot find the melody in my voice.
Whatever I want to say, my words stop half way—
My heart knows defeat and cries—
You've caught me in such a snare
Weaving this web of melody all around.

৪ 4

আমার সকল অঙ্গে তোমার পরশ
লগ্ন হয়ে রহিয়াছে রজনী-দিবস
প্রাণেশ্বর, এই কথা নিত্য মনে আনি
রাখিব পবিত্র করি মোর তনুখানি।
মনে তুমি বিরাজিছ, হে পরম জ্ঞান,
এই কথা সদা স্মরি মোর সর্বধ্যান
সর্বচিন্তা হতে আমি সর্বচেষ্টা করি
সর্বমিথ্যা রাখি দিব দূরে পরিহরি।

হৃদয়ে রয়েছে তব অচল আসন
এই কথা মনে রেখে করিব শাসন
সকল কুটিল দ্বেষ, সর্ব অমঙ্গল—
প্রেমেরে রাখিব করি প্রস্ফুট নির্মল।
সর্ব কর্মে তব শক্তি এই জেনে সার,
করিব সকল কর্মে তোমারে প্রচার।

◆ ◆ ◆

LIFE of my life, I shall ever try to keep my body pure, knowing that thy living touch is upon all my limbs.

I shall ever try to keep all untruths out from my thoughts, knowing that thou art that truth which has kindled the light of reason in my mind.

I shall ever try to drive all evils away from my heart and keep my love in flower, knowing that thou hast thy seat in the inmost shrine of my heart.

And it shall be my endeavour to reveal thee in my actions, knowing it is thy power gives me strength to act.

◆ ◆ ◆

Remembering always that your touch
Is on my limbs night and day,
Lord of my life, I will keep pure
This body of mine.
You reign in my mind, O supreme knowledge,
This I always recall in every meditation
With every thought I will make every effort
To renounce and keep away every falsehood.

Your immovable throne is in my heart
I will remember that and suppress
All that is harsh, all inauspicious—
I'll keep love pure and ever abloom.
Knowing that your strength is in all my actions,
In every action it is you I will express.

৫ 5

তুমি একটু কেবল বসতে দিয়ো কাছে
আমায় শুধু ক্ষণেক তরে।
আজি হাতে আমার যা কিছু কাজ আছে
আমি সাঙ্গ করব পরে।
না চাহিলে তোমার মুখপানে
হৃদয় আমার বিরাম নাহি জানে,
কাজের মাঝে ঘুরে বেড়াই যত
ফিরি কূলহারা সাগরে।

বসন্ত আজ উচ্ছ্বাসে নিশ্বাসে
এল আমার বাতায়নে।
অলস ভ্রমর গুঞ্জরিয়া আসে
ফেরে কুঞ্জের প্রাঙ্গণে।
আজকে শুধু একান্তে আসীন
চোখে চোখে চেয়ে থাকার দিন,
আজকে জীবন-সমর্পণের গান
গাব নীরব অবসরে।

◆ ◆ ◆

I ASK for a moment's indulgence to sit by thy side. The works that I have in hand I will finish afterwards.

Away from the sight of thy face my heart knows no rest nor respite, and my work becomes an endless toil in a shoreless sea of toil.

To-day the summer has come at my window with its sighs and murmurs; and the bees are plying their minstrelsy at the court of the flowering grove.

Now it is time to sit quiet, face to face with thee, and to sing dedication of life in this silent and overflowing leisure.

• • •

Only let me sit
A few moments near you.
Whatever work I have in hand today
I will finish later.
If I cannot look at your face
My heart knows no rest,
I wander about in the midst of work
Turning on a shoreless sea.

Today at my window the breath of spring
Has arrived in all its passion.
The lazy bees come humming and wander
The courtyards of garden and grove.
Today's the day to sit secluded
Only gazing eye to eye.
A song of dedicating my life
I'll sing in this silent leisure today.

৬ 6

ছিন্ন করে লও হে মোরে
আর বিলম্ব নয়।
ধুলায় পাছে ঝরে পড়ি
এই জাগে মোর ভয়।
এ ফুল তোমার মালার মাঝে
ঠাঁই পাবে কি, জানি না যে,
তবু তোমার আঘাতটি তার
ভাগ্যে যেন রয়।
ছিন্ন করো ছিন্ন করো
আর বিলম্ব নয়।

কখন্ যে দিন ফুরিয়ে যাবে,
আসবে আঁধার করে,
কখন্ তোমার পূজার বেলা
কাটবে অগোচরে।
যেটুকু এর রঙ ধরেছে,
গন্ধে সুধায় বুক ভরেছে,
তোমার সেবায় লও সেটুকু
থাকতে সুসময়।
ছিন্ন করো ছিন্ন করো
আর বিলম্ব নয়।

• • •

PLUCK this little flower and take it, delay not! I fear lest it droop and drop into the dust.

It may not find a place in thy garland, but honour it with a touch of pain from thy hand and pluck it. I fear lest the day end before I am aware, and the time of offering go by.

Though its colour be not deep and its smell be

faint, use this flower in thy service and pluck it while there is time.

• • •

Oh, pluck and take me now
        No more delay.
Lest I wither and fall in the dust
        This fear's growing in me.
I don't know if this flower
Will find a place in your garland,
But still, let the pain at your hand
        Be its fortune.
Pluck it now pluck it now
        No more delay.

Who knows when the day might end,
        Darkness come around,
When the time for worship of you
        Pass unknown.
Whatever little color it's caught,
Whatever fragrance or nectar's filled its heart,
Take that little for your service
        While there is time.
Pluck it now pluck it now
        No more delay.

৭ 7

আমার এ গান ছেড়েছে তার
সকল অলংকার,
তোমার কাছে রাখে নি আর
সাজের অহংকার।
অলংকার যে মাঝে প'ড়ে
মিলনেতে আড়াল করে,
তোমার কথা ঢাকে যে তার
মুখর ঝংকার।

তোমার কাছে খাটে না মোর
কবির গরব করা,
মহাকবি, তোমার পায়ে
দিতে চাই যে ধরা।
জীবন লয়ে যতন করি'
যদি সরল বাঁশি গড়ি,
আপন সুরে দিবে ভরি
সকল ছিদ্র তার।

• • •

My song has put off her adornments. She has no pride of dress and decoration. Ornaments would mar our union; they would come between thee and me; their jingling would drown thy whispers.

My poet's vanity dies in shame before thy sight. O master poet, I have sat down at thy feet. Only let me make my life simple and straight, like a flute of reed for thee to fill with music.

• • •

This song of mine has shed
  All its ornament
Hasn't kept its dressed-up conceit
  With you.
Ornaments would come between us
Obstruct our meeting,
Their harsh jangle smother
  Your words.

With you, my poet's pride
  Does not suit.
Master poet, I wish to claim
  My place at your feet.
I'll take my life and try
To make a simple flute, if I can,
That you may fill all its holes
  With your own melody.

৮ ৪

রাজার মতো বেশে তুমি সাজাও যে শিশুরে,
পরাও যারে মণিরতন-হার—
খেলাধুলা আনন্দ তার সকলি যায় ঘুরে,
বসন-ভূষণ হয় যে বিষম ভার।
ছেঁড়ে পাছে আঘাত লাগি,
পাছে ধুলায় হয় সে দাগি,
আপনাকে তাই সরিয়ে রাখে সবার হতে দূরে,
চলতে গেলে ভাবনা ধরে তার—
রাজার মতো বেশে তুমি সাজাও যে শিশুরে,
পরাও যারে মণিরতন-হার।

কী হবে মা অমনতরো রাজার মতো সাজে,
কী হবে ওই মণিরতন-হারে।
দুয়ার খুলে দাও যদি তো ছুটি পথের মাঝে
রৌদ্রবায়ু-ধুলাকাদার পাড়ে।
যেথায় বিশ্বজনের মেলা
সমস্ত দিন নানান খেলা,
চারি দিকে বিরাট গাথা বাজে হাজার সুরে,
সেথায় সে যে পায় না অধিকার,
রাজার মতো বেশে তুমি সাজাও যে শিশুরে,
পরাও যারে মণিরতন-হার।

• • •

THE child who is decked with prince's robes and who has jewelled chains round his neck loses all pleasure in his play; his dress hampers him at every step.

In fear that it may be frayed, or stained with dust he keeps himself from the world, and is afraid even to move.

Mother, it is no gain, thy bondage of finery, if it keep one shut off from the healthful dust of the earth, if it rob one of the right of entrance to the great fair of common human life.

◆ ◆ ◆

The child you adorn with kingly attire,
Whom you give jeweled necklaces to wear—
His play his delight are all turned around,
So heavy are his dress and ornaments.
Lest they be torn or broken,
Lest they be marred with dust,
He keeps himself far from everyone else,
Stopped by his concern before he even moves—
The child you adorn with kingly attire,
Whom you give jeweled necklaces to wear.

What use will it be, mother, this kingly attire,
What use will they be, these jeweled necklaces.
Open the door, and he will run into the street
Into sun, air, dust, and mud.
Into the fair of the world's people
And various games all day long,
On all sides the great ballad sounds a thousand melodies,
But there he finds no right to enter,
The child you adorn with kingly attire,
Whom you give jeweled necklaces to wear.

৯ 9

আর আমায় আমি নিজের শিরে
বইব না।
আর নিজের দ্বারে কাঙাল হয়ে
রইব না।
এই বোঝা তোমার পায়ে ফেলে
বেরিয়ে পড়ব অবহেলে—
কোনো খবর রাখব না ওর,
কোনো কথাই কইব না।
আমায় আমি নিজের শিরে
বইব না।

বাসনা মোর যারেই পরশ
করে সে,
আলোটি তার নিবিয়ে ফেলে
নিমেষে।
ওরে সেই অশুচি, দুই হাতে তার
যা এনেছে চাই নে সে আর
তোমার প্রেমে বাজবে না যা
সে আর আমি সইব না।
আমায় আমি নিজের শিরে
বইব না।

◆ ◆ ◆

O FOOL, to try to carry thyself upon thy own shoulders! O beggar, to come to beg at thy own door!

Leave all thy burdens on his hands who can bear all, and never look behind in regret.

Thy desire at once puts out the light from the

lamp it touches with its breath. It is unholy—take not thy gifts through its unclean hands. Accept only what is offered by sacred love.*

◆ ◆ ◆

No more will I carry myself
upon my own back.
No more will I remain a pauper
at my own door.
Leaving this burden at your feet
I'll set out without a care—
I won't take any notice of it
I won't say a word.
I won't carry myself
upon my own back.

My desire will touch it,
it will,
Putting out its light
in an instant.
Oh, that's unholy, what it brings me
In its cupped hands, I don't want any
more,
Whatever doesn't ring with your love
I won't bear any more.
I won't carry myself
upon my own back.

* Rabindranath uses the second person in his translation, enhancing the power of the poem.

১০ 10

যেথায় থাকে সবার অধম দীনের হতে দীন
সেইখানে যে চরণ তোমার রাজে
সবার পিছে, সবার নীচে,
সব-হারাদের মাঝে।
যখন তোমায় প্রণাম করি আমি,
প্রণাম আমার কোন্‌খানে যায় থামি,
তোমার চরণ যেথায় নামে অপমানের তলে
সেথায় আমার প্রণাম নামে না যে
সবার পিছে, সবার নীচে,
সব-হারাদের মাঝে।

অহংকার তো পায় না নাগাল যেথায় তুমি ফের'
রিক্তভূষণ দীনদরিদ্র সাজে—
সবার পিছে, সবার নীচে,
সব-হারাদের মাঝে।
ধনে মানে যেথায় আছে ভরি
সেথায় তোমার সঙ্গ আশা করি—
সঙ্গী হয়ে আছ যেথায় সঙ্গীহীনের ঘরে
সেথায় আমার হৃদয় নামে না যে
সবার পিছে, সবার নীচে,
সব-হারাদের মাঝে।

• • •

HERE is thy footstool and there rest thy feet where live the poorest, and lowliest, and lost.

When I try to bow to thee, my obeisance cannot reach down to the depth where thy feet rest among the poorest, and lowliest, and lost.

Pride can never approach to where thou walkest in the clothes of the humble among the poorest, and lowliest, and lost.

My heart can never find its way to where thou keepest company with the companionless among the poorest, the lowliest, and the lost.

♦ ♦ ♦

Where the lowest of all are, the poorest of the poor
That's where your feet will stay
Behind them all, beneath them all,
Among the lost-everythings.
When I try to bow down to you,
Somewhere my bow is halted,
Where your feet descend, lower than all ignominy,
So low I cannot bow
Behind them all, beneath them all,
Among the lost-everythings.

Pride cannot reach where you wander,
Without ornament, dressed like the humble poor—
Behind them all, beneath them all,
Among the lost-everythings.
Where all is filled with wealth and honor
There I hope for your company—
Where you are a companion in the homes of those
without company
There my heart cannot descend
Behind them all, beneath them all,
Among the lost-everythings.

১১ 11

ভজন পূজন সাধন আরাধনা
সমস্ত থাক্ পড়ে।
রুদ্ধদ্বারে দেবালয়ের কোণে
কেন আছিস ওরে।
অন্ধকারে লুকিয়ে আপন মনে
কাহারে তুই পূজিস সংগোপনে,
নয়ন মেলে দেখ দেখি তুই চেয়ে
দেবতা নাই ঘরে।

তিনি গেছেন যেথায় মাটি ভেঙে
করছে চাষা চাষ—
পাথর ভেঙে কাটছে যেথায় পথ,
খাটছে বারো মাস।
রৌদ্রে জলে আছেন সবার সাথে,
ধুলা তাঁহার লেগেছে দুই হাতে;
তাঁরি মতন শুচি বসন ছাড়ি
আয় রে ধুলার 'পরে।

মুক্তি? ওরে মুক্তি কোথায় পাবি,
মুক্তি কোথায় আছে।
আপনি প্রভু সৃষ্টিবাঁধন প'রে
বাঁধা সবার কাছে।
রাখো রে ধ্যান, থাক্ রে ফুলের ডালি,
ছিঁড়ুক বস্ত্র, লাগুক ধুলাবালি,
কর্মযোগে তাঁর সাথে এক হয়ে
ঘর্ম পড়ুক ঝরে।

• • •

Leave this chanting and singing and telling of beads! Whom dost thou worship in this lonely dark corner of a temple with doors all shut? Open thine eyes and see thy God is not before thee!

He is there where the tiller is tilling the hard ground and where the path-maker is breaking stones. He is with them in sun and in shower, and his garment is covered with dust. Put off thy holy mantle and even like him come down on the dusty soil!

Deliverance? Where is this deliverance to be found? Our master himself has joyfully taken upon him the bonds of creation; he is bound with us all for ever.

Come out of thy meditations and leave aside thy flowers and incense! What harm is there if thy clothes become tattered and stained? Meet him and stand by him in toil and in sweat of thy brow.

◆ ◆ ◆

The chanting the worship the austerities the prayers
    Leave it all alone.
Oh, why do you stay in a corner of a temple
    With its doors shut.
Hiding in the dark, whom do you worship
In your mind, in secret,
Open your eyes and look around
    God isn't in the room.

He's gone where the farmer breaks ground
    To farm his land—
Where he breaks stone to cut out a path,
    Toils all twelve months.
In sun and in rain he's with everyone,
Both his hands are coated with dust;

Like him, leave off your virtuous cloth
And come down to the dust.

Deliverance? Oh hey, where will you find deliverance,
Where does this deliverance exist.
Our lord himself has taken on the bonds of creation
And is bound to everyone.
Leave your meditations, let the flowers be,
Let your clothes be torn, smeared with dust and sand,
Let your drops of sweat fall
Join with him in devoted toil.

১২ 12

অনেককালের যাত্রা আমার
অনেক দূরের পথে,
প্রথম বাহির হয়েছিলেম
প্রথম-আলোর রথে।
গ্রহে তারায় বেঁকে বেঁকে
পথের চিহ্ন এলেম এঁকে
কত যে লোক-লোকান্তরের
অরণ্যে পর্বতে।

সবার চেয়ে কাছে আসা
সবার চেয়ে দূর।
বড়ো কঠিন সাধনা, যার
বড়ো সহজ সুর।
পরের দ্বারে ফিরে, শেষে
আসে পথিক আপন দেশে—
বাহির-ভুবন ঘুরে মেলে
অন্তরের ঠাকুর।

"এই যে তুমি" এই কথাটি
বলব আমি ব'লে
কত দিকেই চোখ ফেরালেম
কত পথেই চ'লে।
ভরিয়ে জগৎ লক্ষ ধারায়
"আছ-আছ"র স্রোত বহে যায়
"কই তুমি কই" এই কাঁদনের
নয়ন-জলে গ'লে।

• • •

THE time that my journey takes is long and the way of it long.

Poem 12

I came out on the chariot of the first gleam of light, and pursued my voyage through the wildernesses of worlds leaving my track on many a star and planet.

It is the most distant course that comes nearest to thyself, and that training is the most intricate which leads to the utter simplicity of a tune.

The traveller has to knock at every alien door to come to his own, and one has to wander through all the outer worlds to reach the innermost shrine at the end.

My eyes strayed far and wide before I shut them and said "Here art thou!"

The question and the cry "Oh, where?" melt into tears of a thousand streams and deluge the world with the flood of the assurance "I am!"

◆ ◆ ◆

My journey lasts many ages
        And its path is long,
I set out first
        On the chariot of first light.
I traced my path turning
Turning among the planets and stars
Through so many worlds and wildernesses
        Forests and mountains.

To come closest of all
        Is the most distant of all.
It's very rigorous practice
        That finds a very simple melody.

Having gone to every stranger's door, at last
The traveler comes to his own land—
Wandering the outer world outside yields
    The lord within.

"Here you are!" I wanted to say
    And to say this
I walked so many paths
    And gazed so many ways.
Flooding the world with a million streams
The river of "You are—you are" flows on
Merging into the tears of the cry
    "Where are you, where?"

১৩ 13

হেথা যে গান গাইতে আসা আমার
হয় নি সে গান গাওয়া—
আজো কেবলই সুর সাধা, আমার
কেবল গাইতে চাওয়া।

আমার লাগে নাই সে সুর, আমার
বাঁধে নাই সে কথা,
শুধু প্রাণেরই মাঝখানে আছে
গানের ব্যাকুলতা।
আজো ফোটে নাই সে ফুল, শুধু
বহেছে এক হাওয়া।

আমি দেখি নাই তার মুখ, আমি
শুনি নাই তার বাণী,
কেবল শুনি ক্ষণে ক্ষণে তাহার
পায়ের ধ্বনিখানি।
আমার দ্বারের সমুখ দিয়ে সে জন
করে আসা-যাওয়া।

শুধু আসন পাতা হল আমার
সারাটি দিন ধ'রে—
ঘরে হয় নি প্রদীপ জ্বালা, তারে
ডাকব কেমন ক'রে।
আছি পাবার আশা নিয়ে, তারে
হয় নি আমার পাওয়া।

• • •

THE song that I came to sing remains unsung to this day.

I have spent my days in stringing and in unstringing my instrument.

The time has not come true, the words have not been rightly set; only there is the agony of wishing in my heart.

The blossom has not opened; only the wind is sighing by.

I have not seen his face, nor have I listened to his voice; only I have heard his gentle footsteps from the road before my house.

The livelong day has passed in spreading his seat on the floor; but the lamp has not been lit and I cannot ask him into my house.

I live in the hope of meeting with him; but this meeting is not yet.

◆ ◆ ◆

The song that I came here to sing
Is not yet sung.
Even now I only try out the melody, only
Long to sing.

I haven't set the tune, I haven't
Fixed upon the words,
Only the restlessness of song
Stirs within my heart.
Even now that flower hasn't bloomed, only
A breeze has blown.

I haven't seen his face, I
Haven't heard his voice,
I only hear from moment to moment
His footsteps echoing.
As though he comes and goes
In front of my door.

Poem 13

I’ve only   set out his seat
Through all this day,
The lamp   hasn’t been lit in the house, how can I
Call him in.
I live   with the hope of getting him, I
Haven’t got him yet.

১৪ 14

আমি বহু বাসনায় প্রাণপণে চাই,
বঞ্চিত করে বাঁচালে মোরে।
এ কৃপা কঠোর সঞ্চিত মোর
জীবন ভ'রে।
না চাহিতে মোরে যা করেছ দান—
আকাশ আলোক তনু মন প্রাণ,
দিনে দিনে তুমি নিতেছ আমায়
সে মহাদানেরই যোগ্য করে
অতি-ইচ্ছার সংকট হতে
বাঁচায়ে মোরে।

আমি কখনো-বা ভুলি, কখনো-বা চলি
তোমার পথের লক্ষ্য ধরে;
তুমি নিষ্ঠুর সম্মুখ হতে
যাও যে সরে।
এ যে তব দয়া জানি জানি হায়,
নিতে চাও ব'লে ফিরাও আমায়,
পূর্ণ করিয়া লবে এ জীবন
তব মিলনেরই যোগ্য করে
আধা-ইচ্ছার সংকট হতে
বাঁচায়ে মোরে।

• • •

My desires are many and my cry is pitiful, but ever didst thou save me by hard refusals; and this strong mercy has been wrought into my life through and through.

Day by day thou art making me worthy of the simple, great gifts that thou gavest to me unasked—this sky and the light, this body and the life and the mind—saving me from perils of overmuch desire.

Poem 14

There are times when I languidly linger and times when I awaken and hurry in search of my goal; but cruelly thou hidest thyself from before me.

Day by day thou art making me worthy of thy full acceptance by refusing me ever and anon, saving me from perils of weak, uncertain desire.

◆ ◆ ◆

I have many desires I long for with all my heart,
You save me by keeping them from me.
This hard mercy has been gathered
All my life.
Without my asking, you have given me such gifts—
Sky and light, body and mind and life,
Making me more worthy
Of those great gifts day by day,
Saving me from the danger
Of desiring too much.

I forget sometimes, sometimes I walk
Towards my goal, the path to you;
You move away, merciless, from coming
Face to face.
This is your kindness, that I know, I know, alas,
You turn me aside because you want to
receive me,
You will fill this life, making it
Worthy of union with you,
Saving me from the danger
Of a half-formed desire.

১৫ 15

আমি হেথায় থাকি শুধু
গাইতে তোমার গান,
দিয়ো তোমার জগৎসভায়
এইটুকু মোর স্থান।
আমি তোমার ভুবন-মাঝে
লাগি নি নাথ, কোনো কাজে—
শুধু কেবল সুরে বাজে
অকাজের এই প্রাণ।

নিশায় নীরব দেবালয়ে
তোমার আরাধন,
তখন মোরে আদেশ কোরো
গাইতে হে রাজন্।
ভোরে যখন আকাশ জুড়ে
বাজবে বীণা সোনার সুরে
আমি যেন না রই দূরে
এই দিয়ো মোর মান।

• • •

I AM here to sing thee songs. In this hall of thine I have a corner seat.

In thy world I have no work to do; my useless life can only break out in tunes without a purpose.

When the hour strikes for thy silent worship at the dark temple of midnight, command me, my master, to stand before thee to sing.

When in the morning air the golden harp is tuned, honour me, commanding my presence.

• • •

Poem 15

I only remain here
To sing songs of you,
In this hall of your universe
Give me a little space.
In the midst of your world
I haven't set to any work, my lord—
It only resounds to melody
This useless life of mine.

At night in the silent temple,
When you are worshipped,
Then, O master,
Command me to sing.
When at dawn the veena plays
Its golden melody across the sky,
Let me not be far from you
Allow me this honor.

১৬ 16

জগতে আনন্দযজ্ঞে আমার নিমন্ত্রণ।
ধন্য হল ধন্য হল মানবজীবন।
নয়ন আমার রূপের পুরে
সাধ মিটায়ে বেড়ায় ঘুরে,
শ্রবণ আমার গভীর সুরে
হয়েছে মগন।

তোমার যজ্ঞে দিয়েছ ভার
বাজাই আমি বাঁশি।
গানে গানে গেঁথে বেড়াই
প্রাণের কান্নাহাসি।
এখন সময় হয়েছে কি
সভায় গিয়ে তোমায় দেখি
জয়ধ্বনি শুনিয়ে যাব
এ মোর নিবেদন।

⬩ ⬩ ⬩

I HAVE had my invitation to this world's festival, and thus my life has been blessed. My eyes have seen and my ears have heard.

It was my part at this feast to play upon my instrument, and I have done all I could.

Now, I ask, has the time come at last when I may go in and see thy face and offer thee my silent salutation?

⬩ ⬩ ⬩

I am invited to the world's joyful festival.
Blessed, blessed is man's life.
        In beauty's realm, my eyes
        Wander about, drink their fill,
        My hearing is enchanted
                With deep melody.

At your festival, you've given me this duty
        That I play my flute.
Wandering, I string life's tears and laughter
        On song upon song.
                Is it time now
                To enter this assembly and see you
                And hail your reign—
                        This is my offering.

১৭ 17

প্রেমের হাতে ধরা দেব
তাই রয়েছি বসে;
অনেক দেরি হয়ে গেল,
দোষী অনেক দোষে।
বিধিবিধান-বাঁধনডোরে
ধরতে আসে, যাই যে সরে,
তার লাগি যা শাস্তি নেবার
নেব মনের তোষে।
প্রেমের হাতে ধরা দেব
তাই রয়েছি বসে।

লোকে আমায় নিন্দা করে,
নিন্দা সে নয় মিছে,
সকল নিন্দা মাথায় ধরে
রব সবার নীচে।
শেষ হয়ে যে গেল বেলা,
ভাঙল বেচা-কেনার মেলা,
ডাকতে যারা এসেছিল
ফিরল তারা রোষে।
প্রেমের হাতে ধরা দেব
তাই রয়েছি বসে।

◆ ◆ ◆

I AM only waiting for love to give myself up at last into his hands. That is why it is so late and why I have been guilty of such omissions.

They come with their laws and their codes to bind me fast; but I evade them ever, for I am only waiting for love to give myself up at last into his hands.

People blame me and call me heedless; I doubt not they are right in their blame.

Poem 17

The market day is over and work is all done for the busy. Those who came to call me in vain have gone back in anger. I am only waiting for love to give myself up at last into his hands.

◆ ◆ ◆

I only wait to give myself
Into the hands of love;
It's very late now,
I'm at fault for many faults.
With binding-cords of rules and laws
They come to snare me, but I move away,
Whatever punishment I get for that
I'll take and be content.
I only wait to give myself
Into the hands of love.

People censure me,
That censure is not untrue,
I'll take all the censure upon my head
And remain beneath them all.
The day draws to an end,
The fair of buying and selling breaks up,
Those who came to call me
They go back in anger.
I only wait to give myself
Into the hands of love.

১৮ 18

মেঘের 'পরে মেঘ জমেছে,
আঁধার করে আসে,
আমায় কেন বসিয়ে রাখ
একা দ্বারের পাশে।
কাজের দিনে নানা কাজে
থাকি নানা লোকের মাঝে,
আজ আমি যে বসে আছি
তোমারি আশ্বাসে।
আমায় কেন বসিয়ে রাখ
একা দ্বারের পাশে।

তুমি যদি না দেখা দাও,
কর আমায় হেলা,
কেমন করে কাটে আমার
এমন বাদল-বেলা।
দূরের পানে মেলে আঁখি
কেবল আমি চেয়ে থাকি,
পরান আমার কেঁদে বেড়ায়
দুরন্ত বাতাসে।
আমায় কেন বসিয়ে রাখ
একা দ্বারের পাশে।

• • •

CLOUDS heap upon clouds and it darkens. Ah, love, why dost thou let me wait outside at the door all alone?

In the busy moments of the noontide work I am with the crowd, but on this dark lonely day it is only for thee that I hope.

Poem 18

If thou showest me not thy face, if thou leavest me wholly aside, I know not how I am to pass these long, rainy hours.

I keep gazing on the far away gloom of the sky, and my heart wanders wailing with the restless wind.

• • •

Clouds are piled upon clouds,
The dark draws in,
Why do you leave me sitting
Alone by the door.
On a workday, with many tasks
I am amidst many people,
But today I sit
Heartened with hope for you.
Why do you leave me sitting
Alone by the door.

If you don't show yourself
And neglect me,
How will these pass,
My cloud-filled hours.
With my eyes on the distance
I only sit and stare,
My heart crying wanders
On the frenzied air.
Why do you leave me sitting
Alone by the door.

১৯ 19

ওগো মৌন, না যদি কও
না-ই কহিলে কথা।
বক্ষ ভরি বইব আমি
তোমার নীরবতা।
স্তব্ধ হয়ে রইব পড়ে,
রজনী রয় যেমন করে
জ্বালিয়ে তারা নিমেষহারা
ধৈর্যে অবনতা।

হবে হবে প্রভাত হবে
আঁধার যাবে কেটে।
তোমার বাণী সোনার ধারা
পড়বে আকাশ ফেটে।
তখন আমার পাখির বাসায়
জাগবে কি গান তোমার ভাষায়।
তোমার তানে ফোটাবে ফুল
আমার বনলতা?

• • •

If thou speakest not I will fill my heart with thy silence and endure it. I will keep still and wait like the night with starry vigil and its head bent low with patience.

The morning will surely come, the darkness will vanish, and thy voice pour down in golden streams breaking through the sky.

Then thy words will take wing in songs from every one of my birds' nests, and thy melodies will break forth in flowers in all my forest groves.

Poem 19

◆ ◆ ◆

Oh silent one, if you won't speak
        That's fine, don't say a word
I'll fill my chest with your silence
        And bear it with me.
                I'll remain here motionless,
                As the night remains
                Once it's lit its unblinking stars
                        And bowed its head in patience.

It'll come, it'll come, the dawn will come
        The darkness will pass.
Your voice a stream of gold
        Will burst the sky open and pour down.
                Then will the songs in your language
                Rise from my bird's nest?
                Your melodies set the flowers to bloom
                        On my forest vines?

২০ 20

যেদিন ফুটল কমল কিছুই জানি নাই
আমি ছিলেম অন্যমনে।
আমার সাজিয়ে সাজি তারে আনি নাই
সে যে রইল সংগোপনে।
মাঝে মাঝে হিয়া আকুলপ্রায়,
স্বপন দেখে চম্‌কে উঠে চায়,
মন্দ মধুর গন্ধ আসে হায়
কোথায় দখিন-সমীরণে।

ওগো সেই সুগন্ধে ফিরায় উদাসিয়া
আমায় দেশে দেশান্তে।
যেন সন্ধানে তার উঠে নিশ্বাসিয়া
ভুবন নবীন বসন্তে।
কে জানিত দূরে তো নেই সে,
আমারি গো আমারি সেই যে,
এ মাধুরী ফুটেছে হায় রে
আমার হৃদয়-উপবনে।

• • •

On the day when the lotus bloomed, alas, my mind was straying, and I knew it not. My basket was empty and the flower remained unheeded.

Only now and again a sadness fell upon me, and I started up from my dream and felt a sweet trace of a strange fragrance in the south wind.

That vague sweetness made my heart ache with longing and it seemed to me that it was the eager breath of the summer seeking for its completion.

Poem 20

I knew not then that it was so near, that it was mine, and that this perfect sweetness had blossomed in the depth of my own heart.

◆ ◆ ◆

The day the lotus bloomed, I knew nothing of it
I was other-minded.
I didn't bring it set on a tray with trimmings
It remained unheeded.
Now and then my heart grew restless
I would start from my dream and stare,
For a sweet, gentle fragrance came to me, oh
From somewhere upon the south wind.

Oh, that fragrance takes me yearning
From land to land's end
As though the world, searching for it,
Breathes deeply of the new spring.
Who knew then it wasn't far away,
It was mine, oh, it was mine, it was.
This sweetness had blossomed, oh, oh,
In my own heart's garden.

২১ 21

এবার ভাসিয়ে দিতে হবে আমার
এই তরী।
তীরে বসে যায় যে বেলা,
মরি গো মরি।
ফুল-ফোটানো সারা ক'রে
বসন্ত যে গেল স'রে,
নিয়ে ঝরা ফুলের ডালা
বলো কী করি।

জল উঠেছে ছলছলিয়ে,
ঢেউ উঠেছে দুলে,
মর্মরিয়ে ঝরে পাতা
বিজন তরুমূলে।
শূন্যমনে কোথায় তাকাস।
সকল বাতাস সকল আকাশ
ওই পারের ওই বাঁশির সুরে
উঠে শিহরি।

• • •

I MUST launch out my boat. The languid hours pass by on the shore—Alas for me!

The spring has done its flowering and taken leave. And now with the burden of faded futile flowers I wait and linger.

The waves have become clamorous, and upon the bank in the shady lane the yellow leaves flutter and fall.

What emptiness do you gaze upon! Do you not feel a thrill passing through the air with the notes of the far away song floating from the other shore?

◆ ◆ ◆

Now I must set my boat
Out on the water.
The day passes as I sit on the bank,
Oh, I am undone.
Finished with blooming its buds
Spring has gone,
Now tell me what to do
With my tray of withered flowers.

The water splashes up
The waves rock high,
The leaves rustle and drop
Beneath the deserted trees.
Where do you stare with your mind vacant?
All the winds all the skies
Shiver with the melody
Of that flute from that other shore.

২২ 22

আজি শ্রাবণঘন-গহন-মোহে
গোপন তব চরণ ফেলে
নিশার মতো নীরব ওহে
সবার দিঠি এড়ায়ে এলে।
প্রভাত আজি মুদেছে আঁখি,
বাতাস বৃথা যেতেছে ডাকি,
নিলাজ নীল আকাশ ঢাকি
নিবিড় মেঘ কে দিল মেলে।

কূজনহীন কাননভূমি,
দুয়ার দেওয়া সকল ঘরে,
একেলা কোন্ পথিক তুমি
পথিকহীন পথের 'পরে।
হে একা সখা, হে প্রিয়তম,
রয়েছে খোলা এ ঘর মম,
সমুখ দিয়ে স্বপনসম
যেয়ো না মোরে হেলায় ঠেলে।

• • •

In the deep shadows of the rainy July, with secret steps, thou walkest, silent as night, eluding all watchers.

To-day the morning has closed its eyes, heedless of the insistent calls of the loud east wind, and a thick veil has been drawn over the ever-wakeful blue sky.

The woodlands have hushed their songs, and doors are all shut at every house. Thou art the solitary wayfarer in this deserted street. Oh my only friend, my best beloved, the gates are open in my house—do not pass by like a dream.

◆ ◆ ◆

Today in July's deep-densely-clouded enchantment
You come with secret footsteps
Silent as the night, oh,
Avoiding everyone's gaze.
Today the dawn closes its eyes,
The breeze keeps calling in vain
Who has spread the thick clouds
To cover the shameless blue sky.

The woodland without its cooing,
Doors shut on all the houses,
Who are you, lone pathfinder,
Upon this deserted path.
Oh my only friend, oh most beloved,
This my house remains open,
Do not push heedlessly past me
And vanish before me like a dream.

২৩ 23

আজি ঝড়ের রাতে তোমার অভিসার,
পরানসখা বন্ধু হে আমার।
আকাশ কাঁদে হতাশ-সম,
নাই যে ঘুম নয়নে মম,
দুয়ার খুলি হে প্রিয়তম,
চাই যে বারে বার।
পরানসখা বন্ধু হে আমার।

বাহিরে কিছু দেখিতে নাহি পাই,
তোমার পথ কোথায় ভাবি তাই।
সুদূর কোন্ নদীর পারে,
গহন কোন্ বনের ধারে,
গভীর কোন্ অন্ধকারে
হতেছ তুমি পার।
পরানসখা বন্ধু হে আমার।

• • •

ART thou abroad on this stormy night on thy journey of love, my friend? The sky groans like one in despair.

I have no sleep to-night. Ever and again I open my door and look out on the darkness, my friend!

I can see nothing before me. I wonder where lies thy path!

By what dim shore of the ink-black river, by what far edge of the frowning forest, through what mazy depth of gloom art thou threading thy course to come to me, my friend?

Poem 23

◆ ◆ ◆

Now on this night of storms, this lover's journey
of yours
My life's companion, oh my friend.
The sky cries as though bereft of hope,
There's no sleep in my eyes,
Oh beloved, I open the door
And stare out again and again,
My life's companion, oh my friend.

I cannot see anything out there,
Where is your path, I wonder.
On the bank of what distant river,
On the edge of which dense forest,
What deep darkness
Are you coming through.
My life's companion, oh my friend.

২৪ 24

দিবস যদি সাঙ্গ হল, না যদি গাহে পাখি,
ক্লান্ত বায়ু না যদি আর চলে—
এবার তবে গভীর করে ফেলো গো মোরে ঢাকি
অতি নিবিড় ঘন তিমিরতলে—
স্বপন দিয়ে গোপনে ধীরে ধীরে
যেমন করে ঢেকেছ ধরণীরে,
যেমন করে ঢেকেছ তুমি মুদিয়া-পড়া আঁখি,
ঢেকেছ তুমি রাতের শতদলে।

পাথেয় যার ফুরায়ে আসে পথের মাঝখানে,
ক্ষতির রেখা উঠেছে যার ফুটে,
বসনভূষা মলিন হল ধুলায় অপমানে,
শকতি যার পড়িতে চায় টুটে—
ঢাকিয়া দিক তাহার ক্ষতব্যথা
করুণাঘন গভীর গোপনতা,
ঘুচায়ে লাজ ফুটাও তারে নবীন উষা-পানে
জুড়ায়ে তারে আঁধার সুধাজলে।

• • •

If the day is done, if birds sing no more, if the wind has flagged tired, then draw the veil of darkness thick upon me, even as thou hast wrapt the earth with the coverlet of sleep and tenderly closed the petals of the drooping lotus at dusk.

From the traveller, whose sack of provisions is empty before the voyage is ended, whose garment is torn and dust-laden, whose strength is exhausted, remove shame and poverty, and renew his life like a flower under the cover of thy kindly night.

Poem 24

◆ ◆ ◆

If the day is ended, if the birds don't sing,
    If the tired wind moves no more—
So now draw thick over me, cover me under
    The silent, dense dark—
        As you've slowly secretly covered the earth
        By giving it dreams,
    As you've covered the drooping eyelids,
        Covered the petals over the lotus at night.

The traveler whose provisions run out midway,
    Whose line of misfortune is etched anew,
Whose clothes are stained by dust and disgrace,
    Whose strength wants to break—
        Let a deep and secret mercy
        Cover up all his wounds and losses,
    Remove all shame, let him blossom in the new dawn
        Drinking of the dark's cooling dew.

২৫ 25

মাঝে মাঝে কভু যবে অবসাদ আসি
অন্তরের আলোক পলকে ফেলে গ্রাসি,
মন্দপদে যবে শ্রান্তি আসে তিল তিল
তোমার পূজার বৃন্ত করে সে শিথিল
ম্রিয়মাণ—তখনো না যেন করি ভয়,
তখনো অটল আশা যেন জেগে রয়
তোমা-পানে।

তোমা-'পরে করিয়া নির্ভর
সে শ্রান্তির রাত্রে যেন সকল অন্তর
নির্ভয়ে অর্পণ করি পথধূলিতলে
নিদ্রারে আহ্বান করি। প্রাণপণ বলে
ক্লান্ত চিত্তে নাহি তুলি ক্ষীণ কলরব
তোমার পূজার অতি দরিদ্র উৎসব।

রাত্রি এনে দাও তুমি দিবসের চোখে,
আবার জাগাতে তারে নবীন আলোকে।

• • •

In the night of weariness let me give myself up to sleep without struggle, resting my trust upon thee.

Let me not force my flagging spirit into a poor preparation for thy worship.

It is thou who drawest the veil of night upon the tired eyes of the day to renew its sight in a fresher gladness of awakening.

• • •

Poem 25

From time to time when lassitude comes
To eclipse my inner light in an instant,
When fatigue comes with soft steps, little by little,
And withers the desire to worship you, makes
Melancholy—let me not be afraid then,
Then let unshakeable hope still awaken
Towards you.

And resting my faith on you
On such fatigued nights let me offer fearless
All my innermost thoughts beneath your foot-dust
And invite sleep. Let me not strive with all my strength
With tired mind to raise a weak chant
In a very poor ceremony for worshipping you.

You bring night upon the eyes of day
To awaken it again in new light.

২৬ 26

সে যে পাশে এসে বসেছিল,
তবু জাগি নি।
কী ঘুম তোরে পেয়েছিল
হতভাগিনী।
এসেছিল নীরব রাতে
বীণাখানি ছিল হাতে,
স্বপনমাঝে বাজিয়ে গেল
গভীর রাগিণী।

জেগে দেখি দখিন-হাওয়া
পাগল করিয়া
গন্ধ তাহার ভেসে বেড়ায়
আঁধার ভরিয়া।
কেন আমার রজনী যায়,
কাছে পেয়ে কাছে না পায়
কেন গো তার মালার পরশ
বুকে লাগে নি।

◆ ◆ ◆

HE came and sat by my side but I woke not. What a cursed sleep it was, O miserable me!

He came when the night was still; he had his harp in his hands, and my dreams became resonant with its melodies.

Alas, why are my nights all thus lost? Ah, why do I ever miss his sight whose breath touches my sleep?

◆ ◆ ◆

Poem 26

Oh he came and sat by me
And still I didn't wake.
What a sleep had hold of you,
Unlucky woman.
He came on a silent night,
His veena was in his hands,
In the midst of dreams he played
His deep melodies.

I wake to find the south wind
Maddening
Its fragrance floats all around
Filling the dark.
Why does my night pass
Having him near, yet not having him,
Why has my chest never felt
The touch of his garland.

২৭ 27

কোথায় আলো, কোথায় ওরে আলো!
বিরহানলে জ্বালো রে তারে জ্বালো।
রয়েছে দীপ না আছে শিখা,
এই কি ভালে ছিল রে লিখা—
ইহার চেয়ে মরণ সে যে ভালো।
বিরহানলে প্রদীপখানি জ্বালো।

বেদনাদূতী গাহিছে, 'ওরে প্রাণ,
তোমার লাগি জাগেন ভগবান।
নিশীথে ঘন অন্ধকারে
ডাকেন তোরে প্রেমাভিসারে,
দুঃখ দিয়ে রাখেন তোর মান।
তোমার লাগি জাগেন ভগবান।'

গগনতল গিয়েছে মেঘে ভরি,
বাদলজল পড়িছে ঝরি ঝরি।
এ ঘোর রাতে কিসের লাগি
পরান মম সহসা জাগি
এমন কেন করিছে মরি মরি।
বাদলজল পড়িছে ঝরি ঝরি।

বিজুলি শুধু ক্ষণিক আভা হানে,
নিবিড়তর তিমির চোখে আনে।
জানি না কোথা অনেক দূরে
বাজিল গান গভীর সুরে,
সকল প্রাণ টানিছে পথপানে।
নিবিড়তর তিমির চোখে আনে।

কোথায় আলো, কোথায় ওরে আলো!
বিরহানলে জ্বালো রে তারে জ্বালো।
ডাকিছে মেঘ, হাঁকিছে হাওয়া—
সময় গেলে হবে না যাওয়া,

নিবিড় নিশা নিকষঘন কালো।
পরান দিয়ে প্রেমের দীপ জ্বালো।

• • •

Light, oh where is the light? Kindle it with the burning fire of desire!

There is the lamp but never a flicker of a flame,—is such thy fate, my heart! Ah, death were better by far for thee!

Misery knocks at thy door, and her message is that thy lord is wakeful, and he calls thee to the love-tryst through the darkness of night.

The sky is overcast with clouds and the rain is ceaseless. I know not what this is that stirs in me,—I know not its meaning.

A moment's flash of lightning drags down a deeper gloom on my sight, and my heart gropes for the path to where the music of the night calls me.

Light, oh where is the light! Kindle it with the burning fire of desire! It thunders and the wind rushes screaming through the void. The night is black as a black stone. Let not the hours pass by in the dark. Kindle the lamp of love with thy life.

• • •

Where's the light oh where's the light!
Light it oh light it with the fire of unmet desire.
    The lamp remains, there's no flame,
    Is this good, this fate thus etched—

Better than this is even death itself
Light that lamp with the fire of unmet desire.

Sorrow's messenger sings, "Oh life,
The lord is awake for your sake.
    At night in the dense dark
    He calls you to the love-tryst
He gives you grief to save your honor.
The lord is awake for your sake."

The sky is filled with clouds,
The rain falls in drip and drizzle,
    For what in this depth of night
    Does my heart suddenly awake
Why does it go faint and flutter.
The rain falls in drip and drizzle.

The lightning flash strikes only for an instant,
Brings a denser dark to the eyes.
    I don't know where in the far distance
    A song plays with a deep melody,
All my heart pulls me towards the path.
Brings a denser dark to the eyes.

Where's the light oh where's the light!
Light it oh light it with the fire of unmet desire.
    The roaring clouds call, the screaming wind commands—
    If the time is gone, I cannot go,
The dense night is black as solid rock.
Light the lamp of love with all your life.

২৮ 28

জড়ায়ে আছে বাধা, ছাড়ায়ে যেতে চাই,
ছাড়াতে গেলে ব্যথা বাজে।
মুক্তি চাহিবারে তোমার কাছে যাই
চাহিতে গেলে মরি লাজে।
জানি হে তুমি মম জীবনে শ্রেয়তম,
এমন ধন আর নাহি যে তোমা-সম,
তবু যা ভাঙাচোরা ঘরেতে আছে পোরা
ফেলিয়া দিতে পারি না যে।

তোমারে আবরিয়া ধুলাতে ঢাকে হিয়া
মরণ আনে রাশি রাশি,
আমি যে প্রাণ ভরি তাদের ঘৃণা করি
তবুও তাই ভালোবাসি।
এতই আছে বাকি, জমেছে এত ফাঁকি,
কত যে বিফলতা, কত যে ঢাকাঢাকি,
আমার ভালো তাই চাহিতে যবে যাই
ভয় যে আসে মনোমাঝে।

• • •

OBSTINATE are the trammels, but my heart aches when I try to break them.

Freedom is all I want, but to hope for it I feel ashamed.

I am certain that priceless wealth is in thee, and that thou art my best friend, but I have not the heart to sweep away the tinsel that fills my room.

The shroud that covers me is a shroud of dust and death; I hate it, yet hug it in love.

My debts are large, my failures great, my shame secret and heavy; yet when I come to ask for my good, I quake in fear lest my prayer be granted.*

◆ ◆ ◆

The roadblocks are all around, I want to break past them,
When I go to break them, my pain resounds.
I go to you to ask for freedom
But asking, I die of shame.
Oh, I know you are the best of my life,
There is no other wealth like you,
Yet the broken, useless things stuffed in my room
Oh, I'm not able to throw them away.

My heart is covered in their dust, hiding you
Bringing death again and again,
Though I loathe them with all my heart
It's still them that I love.
So much remains, so many omissions amassed,
So many failures, so many cover-ups,
So that when I go to ask for my good
Fear fills my mind.

---

* In his translation, Rabindranath explains the last line of the poem.

২৯ 29

আমার নামটা দিয়ে ঢেকে রাখি যারে
মরছে সে এই নামের কারাগারে।
সকল ভুলে যতই দিবারাতি
নামটারে ওই আকাশপানে গাঁথি,
ততই আমার নামের অন্ধকারে
হারাই আমার সত্য আপনারে।

জড়ো করে ধূলির 'পরে ধূলি
নামটারে মোর উচ্চ করে তুলি।
ছিদ্র পাছে হয় রে কোনোখানে
চিত্ত মম বিরাম নাহি মানে,
যতন করি যতই এ মিথ্যারে
ততই আমি হারাই আপনারে।

• • •

He whom I enclose with my name is weeping in this dungeon. I am ever busy building this wall all around; and as this wall goes up into the sky day by day I lose sight of my true being in its dark shadow.

I take pride in this great wall, and I plaster it with dust and sand lest a least hole should be left in this name; and for all the care I take I lose sight of my true being.

• • •

He whom I keep covered with my name
Is dying in the prison of this name.
The more I forget everything and try
Night and day to set this name on the sky,
The more in the darkness of my name
I lose my true me.

Gathering layer of dust 'pon dust
I build my name up high.
For fear of a crack somewhere
My heart doesn't rest at all,
The more care I take of this lie
The more I lose me.

৩০ 30

একলা আমি বাহির হলেম,
তোমার অভিসারে,
সাথে সাথে কে চলে মোর
নীরব অন্ধকারে।
ছাড়াতে চাই অনেক করে
ঘুরে চলি, যাই যে সরে,
মনে করি আপদ গেছে,
আবার দেখি তারে।

ধরণী সে কাঁপিয়ে চলে—
বিষম চঞ্চলতা।
সকল কথার মধ্যে সে চায়
কইতে আপন কথা।
সে যে আমার আমি, প্রভু,
লজ্জা তাহার নাই যে কভু,
তারে নিয়ে কোন্ লাজে বা
যাব তোমার দ্বারে।

• • •

I CAME out alone on my way to my tryst. But who is this that follows me in the silent dark?

I move aside to avoid his presence but I escape him not.

He makes the dust rise from the earth with his swagger; he adds his loud voice to every word that I utter.

He is my own little self, my lord, he knows no shame; but I am ashamed to come to thy door in his company.

• • •

I came out alone,
Headed to our lovers' meeting,
Who walks beside me
In the silent darkness.
I try many ways to get rid of him
I turn and walk, I move aside,
I think the danger's gone,
But I see him again.

He shakes the earth when he walks—
Moving fast and powerful.
Among all the other words he wants
To say his own words.
Oh, he's my own me, lord,
He never has any shame,
I am ashamed to bring him along
As I go to your door.

৩১ 31

'বন্দী, তোরে কে বেঁধেছে
এত কঠিন ক'রে।'

প্রভু আমায় বেঁধেছে যে
বজ্রকঠিন ডোরে।
মনে ছিল সবার চেয়ে
আমিই হব বড়ো,
রাজার কড়ি করেছিলেম
নিজের ঘরে জড়ো।
ঘুম লাগিতে শুয়েছিলেম
প্রভুর শয্যা পেতে,
জেগে দেখি বাঁধা আছি
আপন ভাণ্ডারেতে।

'বন্দী ওগো, কে গড়েছে
বজ্রবাঁধনখানি।'

আপনি আমি গড়েছিলেম
বহু যতন মানি।
ভেবেছিলেম আমার প্রতাপ
করবে জগৎ গ্রাস,
আমি রব একলা স্বাধীন,
সবাই হবে দাস।
তাই গড়েছি রজনীদিন
লোহার শিকলখানা—
কত আগুন কত আঘাত
নাইকো তার ঠিকানা।
গড়া যখন শেষ হয়েছে
কঠিন সুকঠোর,
দেখি আমায় বন্দী করে
আমারি এই ডোর।

• • •

"PRISONER, tell me, who was it that bound you?"

"It was my master," said the prisoner. "I thought I could outdo everybody in the world in wealth and power, and I amassed in my own treasure-house the money due to my king. When sleep overcame me I lay upon the bed that was for my lord, and on waking up I found I was a prisoner in my own treasure-house."

"Prisoner, tell me who was it that wrought this unbreakable chain?"

"It was I," said the prisoner, "who forged this chain very carefully. I thought my invincible power would hold the world captive leaving me in a freedom undisturbed. Thus night and day I worked at the chain with huge fires and cruel hard strokes. When at last the work was done and the links were complete and unbreakable, I found that it held me in its grip."

• • •

"Prisoner, who bound you
So tightly?"

My lord it was who bound me
With these chains hard as stone.
I wanted in my mind
To be larger than everyone else,
In my own house I had amassed
A king's coins.

When sleep came I lay down
Upon my lord's bed
I woke and saw I was bound
In my own treasure-house.

"Oh prisoner, who has forged
These chains hard as stone?"

I made them myself
Taking great care.
I thought my power
Could swallow up the world,
I would alone be free
All others slaves to me.
So I worked night and day
To forge these iron fetters—
So much fire, so many blows
There's no count of them.
When the forging was done
Hard and unbreakable,
I saw these my very own chains
Now held me tight.

৩২ 32

সংসারেতে আর-যাহারা
আমায় ভালোবাসে
তারা আমায় ধরে রাখে
বেঁধে কঠিন পাশে।
তোমার প্রেম যে সবার বাড়া
তাই তোমারি নূতন ধারা,
বাঁধ নাকো, লুকিয়ে থাক'
ছেড়েই রাখ দাসে।

আর-সকলে, ভুলি পাছে
তাই রাখে না একা।
দিনের পরে কাটে যে দিন,
তোমারি নেই দেখা।
তোমায় ডাকি নাই বা ডাকি,
যা খুশি তাই নিয়ে থাকি;
তোমার খুশি চেয়ে আছে
আমার খুশির আশে।

• • •

By all means they try to hold me secure who love me in this world. But it is otherwise with thy love which is greater than theirs, and thou keepest me free.

Lest I forget them they never venture to leave me alone. But day passes by after day and thou art not seen.

If I call not thee in my prayers, if I keep not thee in my heart, thy love for me still waits for my love.

• • •

Poem 32

All the others who love me
    In the world
They hold me close
    And bind me tight.
        But your love is greatest of all
        That's why it's a new kind,
            You don't tie me up, you hide yourself,
            You keep your slave free.

All the others won't leave me alone
    Lest I forget them
But day passes after day
    And you're not to be seen.
        Whether I call you or whether I don't,
        Or I'm busy with whatever pleases me,
            Your happiness waits
            In hope for my happiness.

৩৩ 33

তারা দিনের বেলা এসেছিল
আমার ঘরে,
বলেছিল, একটি পাশে
রইব প'ড়ে।
বলেছিল, দেবতাসেবায়
আমরা হব তোমার সহায়—
যা কিছু পাই প্রসাদ লব
পূজার পরে।

এমনি করে দরিদ্র ক্ষীণ
মলিন বেশে
সংকোচেতে একটি কোণে
রইল এসে।
রাতে দেখি প্রবল হয়ে
পশে আমার দেবালয়ে,
মলিন হাতে পূজার বলি
হরণ করে।

• • •

WHEN it was day they came into my house and said, "We shall only take the smallest room here."

They said, "We shall help you in the worship of your God and humbly accept only our own share of his grace"; and then they took their seat in a corner and they sat quiet and meek.

But in the darkness of night I find they break into my sacred shrine, strong and turbulent, and snatch with unholy greed the offerings from God's altar.

• • •

They came during the daytime
        To my house,
And said, we'll just stay here
        On one side.
They said, in serving the lord
We'll be your helpers—
Whatever blessed offerings we get
        We'll accept after the prayers.

Thus in their poor and meager way
        In their stained clothes
Meek in a corner
        They came and stayed.
At night I see them, grown in power,
Enter my lord's shrine,
Plunder the prayer offerings
        With their stained hands.

৩৪ 34

তোমায় আমার প্রভু করে রাখি
আমার আমি সেইটুকু থাক্ বাকি।
তোমায় আমি হেরি সকল দিশি,
সকল দিয়ে তোমার মাঝে মিশি,
তোমারে প্রেম জোগাই দিবানিশি,
ইচ্ছা আমার সেইটুকু থাক্ বাকি—
তোমায় আমার প্রভু করে রাখি।

তোমায় আমি কোথাও নাহি ঢাকি
কেবল আমার সেইটুকু থাক্ বাকি।
তোমার লীলা হবে এ প্রাণ ভরে
এ সংসারে রেখেছ তাই ধরে,
রইব বাঁধা তোমার বাহুডোরে
বাঁধন আমার সেইটুকু থাক্ বাকি—
তোমায় আমার প্রভু করে রাখি।

◆ ◆ ◆

LET only that little be left of me whereby I may name thee my all.*

Let only that little be left of my will whereby I may feel thee on every side, and come to thee in everything, and offer to thee my love every moment.

Let only that little be left of me whereby I may never hide thee.

Let only that little of my fetters be left whereby I am bound with thy will, and thy purpose is carried out in my life—and that is the fetter of thy love.

---

* Rabindranath translates *probhu* ("lord") as "all," thereby setting up a play with "little" in the first line.

Poem 34

• • •

Let only so little me of myself remain
That I may keep you my lord.
    That I may see you on all sides,
    Yield everything to blend into you,
    Offer you my love day and night,
        Let only that little of my desire remain—
        That I may keep you my lord.

Let only that little of me remain
That I never hide any part of you.
    Your will at play fills my life
    That is why you hold me in this world,
    I'll remain tied to the cord in your hand
        Let only those few of my cords remain—
        That I may keep you my lord.

৩৫ 35

চিত্ত যেথা ভয়শূন্য, উচ্চ যেথা শির,
জ্ঞান যেথা মুক্ত, যেথা গৃহের প্রাচীর
আপন প্রাঙ্গণতলে দিবসশর্বরী
বসুধারে রাখে নাই খণ্ড ক্ষুদ্র করি,
যেথা বাক্য হৃদয়ের উৎসমুখ হতে
উচ্ছ্বসিয়া উঠে, যেথা নির্বারিত স্রোতে
দেশে দেশে দিশে দিশে কর্মধারা ধায়
অজস্র সহস্রবিধ চরিতার্থতায়—

যেথা তুচ্ছ আচারের মরুবালুরাশি
বিচারের স্রোতঃপথ ফেলে নাই গ্রাসি,
পৌরুষেরে করে নি শতধা; নিত্য যেথা
তুমি সর্ব কর্ম চিন্তা আনন্দের নেতা—
নিজ হস্তে নির্দয় আঘাত করি, পিতঃ,
ভারতেরে সেই স্বর্গে করো জাগরিত।

• • •

WHERE the mind is without fear and the head is held high;

Where knowledge is free;

Where the world has not been broken up into fragments by narrow domestic walls;

Where words come out from the depth of truth;

Where tireless striving stretches its arms towards perfection;

Where the clear stream of reason has not lost its way into the dreary desert sand of dead habit;

Where the mind is led forward by thee into ever-widening thought and action—

Into that heaven of freedom, my Father, let my country awake.

Poem 35

• • •

Where the mind is without fear, where the head is high,
Where knowledge is free, where household walls
Do not keep the world broken into tiny pieces
Within their own courtyards day and night,
Where speech bursts out from the heart's fountain,
Where the work-stream flows unrestrained,
Runs from land to land on every side
Towards a thousand different kinds of fulfillment—

Where the desert sand-heaps of trivial custom
Have not swallowed up the stream of reason
And broken manhood a hundred ways; where always
You are the guide in all deed and thought and joy—
Strike hard with your own hand, oh father,
And wake Bharat into that heaven.

৩৬ 36

তব কাছে এই মোর শেষ নিবেদন—
সকল ক্ষীণতা মম করহ ছেদন
দৃঢ়বলে, অন্তরের অন্তর হইতে
প্রভু মোর। বীর্য দেহো সুখের সহিতে,
সুখেরে কঠিন করি। বীর্য দেহো দুখে,
যাহে দুঃখ আপনারে শান্তস্মিত মুখে
পারে উপেক্ষিতে। ভকতিরে বীর্য দেহো
কর্মে যাহে হয় সে সফল, প্রীতি স্নেহ
পুণ্যে ওঠে ফুটি। বীর্য দেহো ক্ষুদ্র জনে
না করিতে হীনজ্ঞান, বলের চরণে
না লুটিতে। বীর্য দেহো চিত্তেরে একাকী
প্রত্যহের তুচ্ছতার ঊর্ধ্বে দিতে রাখি।

বীর্য দেহো তোমার চরণে পাতি শির
অহর্নিশি আপনারে রাখিবারে স্থির।

◆ ◆ ◆

THIS is my prayer to thee, my lord—strike, strike at the root of penury in my heart.

Give me the strength lightly to bear my joys and sorrows.

Give me the strength to make my love fruitful in service.

Give me the strength never to disown the poor or bend my knees before insolent might.

Give me the strength to raise my mind high above daily trifles.

And give me the strength to surrender my strength to thy will with love.

Poem 36

◆ ◆ ◆

This is my final petition to you—
Cut out with your power all the weaknesses
From my innermost depths,
My lord. Give me the strength for happiness
When that happiness is hard. Give me strength
In sorrow, so that sorrow may ignore itself
With a peaceful smiling face. Give devotion
The strength to succeed in its work, and let joy and love
Bloom in virtue. Give me the strength not to think
The poor inferior, or to roll over
At the feet of the powerful. Give me the strength
To raise my mind unaided above the trivial every day.

Give me the strength to lay my head at your feet
And keep myself always resolute.

৩৭ 37

ভেবেছিনু মনে যা হবার তারি শেষে
যাত্রা আমার বুঝি থেমে গেছে এসে।
নাই বুঝি পথ, নাই বুঝি আর কাজ,
পাথেয় যা ছিল ফুরায়েছে বুঝি আজ,
যেতে হবে সরে নীরব অন্তরালে
জীর্ণ জীবনে ছিন্ন মলিন বেশে।

কী নিরখি আজি, এ কী অফুরান লীলা,
এ কী নবীনতা বহে অন্তঃশীলা।
পুরাতন ভাষা মরে এল যবে মুখে,
নবগান হয়ে গুমরি উঠিল বুকে,
পুরাতন পথ শেষ হয়ে গেল যেথা
সেথায় আমারে আনিলে নূতন দেশে।

• • •

I THOUGHT that my voyage had come to its end at the last limit of my power,—that the path before me was closed, that provisions were exhausted and the time come to take shelter in a silent obscurity.

But I find that thy will knows no end in me. And when old words die out on the tongue, new melodies break forth from the heart; and where the old tracks are lost, new country is revealed with its wonders.

• • •

I thought whatever was to happen
Had happened, and my journey had come to an end.
I thought no work remained, no more road to travel,
My supplies had just run out,

And I'd have to move into a silent unknown,
A dried-out life, in torn and dirty clothes.

What do I see today, what is this endless play,
What is this newness that flows in the depth of the heart.
When the old language dies out in the mouth,
Becomes a new song that wells up in the chest
Where the old path comes to an end
There you've brought me to a new land.

চাই গো আমি তোমারে চাই
তোমায় আমি চাই—
এই কথাটি সদাই মনে
বলতে যেন পাই।
আর যা-কিছু বাসনাতে
ঘুরে বেড়াই দিনে রাতে
মিথ্যা সে-সব মিথ্যা, ওগো
তোমায় আমি চাই।

রাত্রি যেমন লুকিয়ে রাখে
আলোর প্রার্থনাই—
তেমনি গভীর মোহের মাঝে
তোমায় আমি চাই।
শান্তিরে ঝড় যখন হানে
শান্তি তবু চায় সে প্রাণে,
তেমনি তোমায় আঘাত করি
তবু তোমায় চাই।

• • •

THAT I want thee, only thee—let my heart repeat without end. All desires that distract me, day and night, are false and empty to the core.

As the night keeps hidden in its gloom the petition for light, even thus in the depth of my unconsciousness rings the cry—I want thee, only thee.

As the storm still seeks its end in peace when it strikes against peace with all its might, even thus my rebellion strikes against thy love and still its cry is—I want thee, only thee.

• • •

I want, oh I want you
        It is you I want—
May I always be able
        To say this in my mind.
With whatever other desires
I wander day and night
Those are false, all false, oh
        It is you I want.

As the night hides
        Its prayer for light—
So within the depth of my world's illusions
        It is you I want.
When the storm shatters the peace
But still wants peace in its heart,
So I strike out against you
        But still want you.

৩৯ 39

জীবন যখন শুকায়ে যায়
করুণাধারায় এসো।
সকল মাধুরী লুকায়ে যায়,
গীতসুধারসে এসো।
কর্ম যখন প্রবল-আকার
গরজি উঠিয়া ঢাকে চারি ধার,
হৃদয়প্রান্তে, হে নীরব নাথ,
শান্তচরণে এসো।

আপনারে যবে করিয়া কৃপণ
কোণে পড়ে থাকে দীনহীন মন,
দুয়ার খুলিয়া, হে উদার নাথ,
রাজসমারোহে এসো।
বাসনা যখন বিপুল ধুলায়
অন্ধ করিয়া অবোধে ভুলায়
ওহে পবিত্র, ওহে অনিদ্র,
রুদ্র আলোকে এসো।

◆ ◆ ◆

WHEN the heart is hard and parched up, come upon me with a shower of mercy.

When grace is lost from life, come with a burst of song.

When tumultuous work raises its din on all sides shutting me out from beyond, come to me, my lord of silence, with thy peace and rest.

When my beggarly heart sits crouched, shut up in a corner, break open the door, my king, and come with the ceremony of a king.

When desire blinds the mind with delusion and dust, O thou holy one, thou wakeful, come with thy light and thy thunder.

◆ ◆ ◆

When life dries out
Come to me in a stream of compassion.
All beauty is hidden,
Come with song's sweet nectar.
When work takes on a mighty form
And thunders and hides everything around
Come, my silent lord, with your quiet footsteps,
Come into my heart's-land.

When my mind has made itself a miser
And lies poor and wretched in a corner,
Open the door, oh generous lord,
Come with the ceremony of a king.
When the vast sandstorm of desire
Blinds me with foolish delusion
Oh holy, oh wakeful one,
Come with your terrible light and thunder.

৪০ 40

দীর্ঘকাল অনাবৃষ্টি, অতি দীর্ঘকাল,
হে ইন্দ্র, হৃদয়ে মম। দিক্‌চক্রবাল
ভয়ংকর শূন্য হেরি, নাই কোনোখানে
সরস সজল রেখা—কেহ নাহি আনে
নববারিবর্ষণের শ্যামল সংবাদ।

যদি ইচ্ছা হয়, দেব, আনো বজ্রনাদ
প্রলয়মুখর হিংস্র ঝটিকার সাথে।
পলে পলে বিদ্যুতের বক্র কশাঘাতে
সচকিত করো মোর দিগ্‌দিগন্তর।
সংহরো সংহরো, প্রভো, নিস্তব্ধ প্রখর
এই রুদ্র, এই ব্যাপ্ত, এ নিঃশব্দ দাহ
নিঃসহ নৈরাশ্যতাপ। চাহো নাথ, চাহো
জননী যেমন চাহে সজল নয়ানে
পিতার ক্রোধের দিনে সন্তানের পানে।

◆ ◆ ◆

THE rain has held back for days and days, my God, in my arid heart. The horizon is fiercely naked—not the thinnest cover of a soft cloud, not the vaguest hint of a distant cool shower.

Send thy angry storm, dark with death, if it is thy wish, and with lashes of lightning startle the sky from end to end.

But call back, my lord, call back this pervading silent heat, still and keen and cruel, burning the heart with dire despair.

Let the cloud of grace bend low from above like the tearful look of the mother on the day of the father's wrath.

◆ ◆ ◆

A long time and no rain, a very long time,
Oh Indra, in my heart. The horizon I see
Terrifying, empty, nowhere does an outline
Show water—nothing brings
The cloud-colored message of a new rainfall.

If you wish, god, bring a thunderclap
And the clamor and destruction of a ferocious storm,
And bent lightning's whip-stroke at every instant
Startle everything every side of me.
Take it back, o master, take back this cutting, motionless,
This terrible, this pervading, this silent, scorching
Heat of helpless despair. Look, lord, look upon me
The way a mother looks with tearful eyes
At a child on the day of a father's rage.

৪১

41

কোথা ছায়ার কোণে দাঁড়িয়ে তুমি কিসের প্রতীক্ষায়
কেন আছ সবার পিছে।
যারা ধুলা-পায়ে ধায় গো পথে, তোমায় ঠেলে যায়,
তারা তোমায় ভাবে মিছে।
আমি তোমার লাগি কুসুম তুলি, বসি তরুর মূলে,
আমি সাজিয়ে রাখি ডালি—
ওগো, যে আসে সেই একটি-দুটি নিয়ে যে যায় তুলে,
আমার সাজি হয় যে খালি।

ওগো, সকাল গেল, বিকাল গেল, সন্ধ্যা হয়ে আসে,
চোখে লাগছে ঘুমঘোর।
সবাই ঘরের পানে যাবার বেলা আমায় দেখে হাসে,
মনে লজ্জা লাগে মোর।
আমি বসে আছি বসনখানি টেনে মুখের 'পরে
যেন ভিখারিনীর মতো—
কেহ শুধায় যদি 'কী চাও তুমি' থাকি নিরুত্তরে
করি দুটি নয়ন নত।

আজি কোন্ লাজে বা বলব আমি 'তোমায় শুধু চাহি',
আমি বলব কেমন করে—
শুধু তোমারি পথ চেয়ে আমি রজনী দিন বাহি,
তুমি আসবে আমার তরে।
আমার দৈন্যখানি যত্নে রাখি, রাজৈশ্বর্যে তব
তারে দিব বিসর্জন—
ওগো, অভাগিনীর এ অভিমান কাহার কাছে কব,
তাহা রইল সংগোপন।

আমি সুদূর-পানে চেয়ে চেয়ে ভাবি আপন-মনে
হেথা তৃণে আসন মেলে—
তুমি হঠাৎ কখন আসবে হেথায় বিপুল আয়োজনে
তোমার সকল আলো জ্বেলে।

তোমার রথের 'পরে সোনার ধ্বজা ঝলবে ঝলমল,
সাথে বাজবে বাঁশির তান—
তোমার প্রতাপ-ভরে বসুন্ধরা করবে টলমল,
আমার উঠবে নেচে প্রাণ!

তখন পথের লোকে অবাক হয়ে সবাই চেয়ে রবে,
তুমি নেমে আসবে পথে;
হেসে দু হাত ধরে ধুলা হতে আমায় তুলে লবে—
তুমি লবে তোমার রথে।
আমার ভূষণবিহীন মলিন বেশে ভিখারিনীর সাজে
তোমার দাঁড়াব বাম পাশে,
তখন লতার মতো কাঁপব আমি গর্বে সুখে লাজে
সকল বিশ্বের সকাশে।

ওগো, সময় বয়ে যাচ্ছে চলে, রয়েছি কান পেতে—
কোথা কই গো চাকার ধ্বনি।
তোমার এ পথ দিয়ে কত-না লোক গর্বে গেল মেতে
কতই জাগিয়ে রনরনি।
তবে তুমিই কি গো নীরব হয়ে রবে ছায়ার তলে,
তুমি রবে সবার শেষে—
হেথায় ভিখারিনীর লজ্জা কী গো ঝরবে নয়নজলে।
তারে রাখবে মলিন বেশে?

• • •

WHERE dost thou stand behind them all, my lover, hiding thyself in the shadows? They push thee and pass thee by on the dusty road, taking thee for naught. I wait here weary hours spreading my offerings for thee, while passers by come and take my flowers, one by one, and my basket is nearly empty.

The morning time is past, and the noon. In the shade of evening my eyes are drowsy with sleep. Men going home glance at me and smile and fill me with shame. I sit like a beggar maid, drawing my skirt over my face, and when they ask me, what it is I want, I drop my eyes and answer them not.

Oh, how, indeed, could I tell them that for thee I wait, and that thou hast promised to come. How could I utter for shame that I keep for my dowry this poverty. Ah, I hug this pride in the secret of my heart.

I sit on the grass and gaze upon the sky and dream of the sudden splendour of thy coming—all the lights ablaze, golden pennons flying over thy car, and they at the roadside standing agape, when they see thee come down from thy seat to raise me from the dust, and set at thy side this ragged beggar girl a-tremble with shame and pride, like a creeper in a summer breeze.

But time glides on and still no sound of the wheels of thy chariot. Many a procession passes by with noise and shouts and glamour of glory. Is it only thou who wouldst stand in the shadow silent and behind them all? And only I who would wait and weep and wear out my heart in vain longing?

◆ ◆ ◆

Where do you stand, and waiting for whom, in a shadowed corner
Why are you behind everyone else?
They who walk the road with dusty feet, they push past you,
They think you aren't there.
I pluck flowers for you, sit beneath the tree,
I arrange the offering-basket—

Poem 41

Oh,   whoever comes takes one or two flowers,
       My basket becomes empty.

Oh,   the morning passes, the afternoon passes,
                    evening comes,
       My eyes are heavy with sleep.
Those going home look at me and laugh,
       My mind fills with shame.
I   sit with my cloth pulled over my face
       Like a beggar woman—
If   anyone asks, "What do you want," I stay silent
       And lower my eyes.

But   with what shame would I say, "I want only you,"
       How can I say that—
I   pass the night and day looking your way,
       Will you come to me?
I   hold my poverty with care, to sink it
       Into your royal glory—
Oh,   whom would I tell of this luckless one's pride,
       I hold this secret close.

I   look and look into the distance and think to myself
       Sitting here on the grass—
When   will you suddenly arrive in your great splendor
       With all your lights ablaze.
On   your chariot flags of gold will shimmer and flash,
       And flute melodies will play—
The   earth will shake with your power,
       My heart will leap up and dance!

Then   all on the road will stare speechless,
       You will step down onto the road.

Smiling, you'll take me by both hands, lift me from the dust—
You'll take me to your chariot.
In my unadorned, stained clothes, dressed like a beggar-woman
I'll stand at your left side,
Trembling like a vine with pride, content, shame
In front of all the world.

Oh time goes flowing by, I wait with ears laid open—
Where is the sound of chariot wheels!
On this your road, how many people pass, frenzied with pride,
With how much fanfare!
Then will you alone remain silent, oh, in the shade,
You remain behind all others—
And here, will the beggar woman's shame flow in tears.
Will you keep her in stained clothes?

৪২ 42

কথা ছিল এক-তরীতে কেবল তুমি আমি
যাব অকারণে ভেসে কেবল ভেসে,
ত্রিভুবনে জানবে না কেউ আমরা তীর্থগামী
কোথায় যেতেছি কোন্ দেশে সে কোন্ দেশে।
কূলহারা সেই সমুদ্র-মাঝখানে
শোনাব গান একলা তোমার কানে,
ঢেউয়ের মতন ভাষা-বাঁধন-হারা
আমার সেই রাগিণী শুনবে নীরব হেসে।

আজো সময় হয় নি কি তার, কাজ কি আছে বাকি।
ওগো ওই-যে সন্ধ্যা নামে সাগরতীরে।
মলিন আলোয় পাখা মেলে সিন্ধুপারের পাখি
আপন কুলায়-মাঝে সবাই এল ফিরে।
কখন তুমি আসবে ঘাটের 'পরে
বাঁধনটুকু কেটে দেবার তরে।
অস্তরবির শেষ আলোটির মতো
তরী নিশীথ-মাঝে যাবে নিরুদ্দেশে।

• • •

Early in the day it was whispered that we should sail in a boat, only thou and I, and never a soul in the world would know of this our pilgrimage to no country and to no end.

In that shoreless ocean, at thy silently listening smile my songs would swell in melodies, free as waves, free from all bondage of words.

Is the time not come yet? Are there works still to do? Lo, the evening has come down upon the shore and in the fading light the seabirds come flying to their nests.

Who knows when the chains will be off, and the boat, like the last glimmer of sunset, vanish into the night?

◆ ◆ ◆

It was fixed, only you and I would go in a boat
    For   no reason, we'd float just float,
No one in the three worlds would know we were pilgrims
    Going somewhere, to what land, to what land.
        In the middle of that shoreless ocean
        I'll sing my songs in your ear alone,
        Like the waves free, free of the limits of language
    You'll   listen to those melodies smiling and silent.

Isn't it time for that yet, does some work still remain.
    Oh   there the evening comes down on the seashore.
In the dimming light the birds from across the river
    Spread their wings and all return to their own nests.
        When will you come to the pier
        To cut off these ties.
        And like the last light of the setting sun
    The   boat will vanish into the night.

৪৩ 43

তখন করি নি, নাথ, কোনো আয়োজন;
বিশ্বের সবার সাথে, হে বিশ্বরাজন্,
অজ্ঞাতে আসিতে হাসি আমার অন্তরে
কত শুভদিনে; কত মুহূর্তের ’পরে
অসীমের চিহ্ন লিখে গেছ! লই তুলি
তোমার স্বাক্ষর-আঁকা সেই ক্ষণগুলি—
দেখি তারা স্মৃতি-মাঝে আছিল ছড়ায়ে
কত-না ধূলির সাথে, আছিল জড়ায়ে
ক্ষণিকের কত তুচ্ছ সুখদুঃখ ঘিরে।

হে নাথ, অবজ্ঞা করি যাও নাই ফিরে
আমার সে ধুলাস্তূপ খেলাঘর দেখে।
খেলা-মাঝে শুনিতে পেয়েছি থেকে থেকে
যে চরণধ্বনি— আজ শুনি তাই বাজে
জগৎসংগীত-সাথে চন্দ্রসূর্য-মাঝে।

• • •

THE day was when I did not keep myself in readiness for thee; and entering my heart unbidden even as one of the common crowd, unknown to me, my king, thou didst press the signet of eternity upon many a fleeting moment of my life.

And to-day when by chance I light upon them and see thy signature, I find they have lain scattered in the dust mixed with the memory of joys and sorrows of my trivial days forgotten.

Thou didst not turn in contempt from my childish play among dust, and the steps that I heard in my playroom are the same that are echoing from star to star.

◆ ◆ ◆

I did not make any preparations then, my lord,
Laughing, you would enter in me unknown,
Like everyone else, O ruler of the world,
On so many lucky days, and set the mark of the eternal
On so many moments! I pick up
Those minutes with your sign on them—
I see they were scattered among memories
Lying in so much dust, tangled
With so many small, fleeting joys and sorrows.

O lord, you did not turn away in contempt
Seeing that dust-heap playroom of mine.
The footsteps I heard from time to time
In my play— today I hear them ring out
Among the moon and the stars with the music of the
universe.

৪৪ 44

আমার এই পথ-চাওয়াতেই
আনন্দ।
খেলে যায় রৌদ্র ছায়া,
বর্ষা আসে।
বসন্ত।
কারা এই সমুখ দিয়ে
আসে যায় খবর নিয়ে,
খুশি রই আপন মনে,
বাতাস বহে
সুমন্দ।

সারাদিন আঁখি মেলে
দুয়ারে রব একা।
শুভখন হঠাৎ এলে
তখনি পাব দেখা।
ততখন ক্ষণে ক্ষণে
হাসি গাই মনে মনে,
ততখন রহি রহি
ভেসে আসে
সুগন্ধ।
আমার এই পথ-চাওয়াতেই
আনন্দ।

• • •

THIS is my delight, thus to wait and watch at the wayside where shadow chases light and the rain comes in the wake of the summer.

Messengers, with tidings from unknown skies, greet me and speed along the road. My heart is glad within, and the breath of the passing breeze is sweet.

From dawn till dusk I sit here before my door, and I know that of a sudden the happy moment will arrive when I shall see.

In the meanwhile I smile and I sing all alone. In the meanwhile the air is filling with the perfume of promise.

◆ ◆ ◆

In watching the road like this
Is my pleasure.
Sunlight and shadow play and pass
Comes the rain.
Springtime.
Who are these who pass by
They come and go, saying hello,
I'm happy within myself,
The breeze blows
Sweet and mild.

All day I'll sit alone
At my door, eyes wide.
When the moment suddenly comes
Only then will I see.
Until then from time to time
I smile and sing to myself,
Until then little by little
Comes floating
A fragrance.
In watching the road like this
Is my pleasure.

৪৫ 45

তোরা শুনিস নি কি শুনিস নি তার পায়ের ধ্বনি,
ওই যে আসে, আসে, আসে।
যুগে যুগে পলে পলে দিন-রজনী
সে যে আসে, আসে, আসে।
গেয়েছি গান যখন যত
আপন-মনে খ্যাপার মতো
সকল সুরে বেজেছে তার
আগমনী—
সে যে আসে, আসে, আসে।

কত কালের ফাগুন-দিনে বনের পথে
সে যে আসে, আসে, আসে।
কত শ্রাবণ-অন্ধকারে মেঘের রথে
সে যে আসে, আসে, আসে।
দুখের পরে পরম দুখে
তারি চরণ বাজে বুকে,
সুখে কখন্ বুলিয়ে সে দেয়
পরশমণি।
সে যে আসে, আসে, আসে।

• • •

HAVE you not heard his silent steps? He comes, comes, ever comes.

Every moment and every age, every day and every night he comes, comes, ever comes.

Many a song have I sung in many a mood of mind, but all their notes have always proclaimed, "He comes, comes, ever comes."

In the fragrant days of sunny April through the forest path he comes, comes, ever comes.

In the rainy gloom of July nights on the thundering chariot of clouds he comes, comes, ever comes.

In sorrow after sorrow it is his steps that press upon my heart, and it is the golden touch of his feet that makes my joy to shine.

• • •

Haven't   you heard, haven't heard his footsteps,
    There he   comes, he comes, he comes.
Age after age moment to moment day and night
    He does   come, he comes, he comes.
                Whenever, however many songs I've sung
                To myself like a madman
                My strings have played all melodies
                        Of welcome—
            He does   come, he comes, he comes.

On springtime days through the ages, on a forest path
    He does   come, he comes, he comes.
In so much monsoon-darkness, on a chariot of clouds
    He does   come, he comes, he comes.
                In sorrow after deepest sorrow,
                It is his steps that sound in my chest,
                His touch unknown on the magic stone
                        That brings happiness.
            He does   come, he comes, he comes.

৪৬ 46

আমার মিলন লাগি তুমি
আসছ কবে থেকে।
তোমার চন্দ্র সূর্য তোমায়
রাখবে কোথায় ঢেকে।
কত কালের সকাল-সাঁঝে
তোমার চরণধ্বনি বাজে,
গোপনে দূত হৃদয়-মাঝে
গেছে আমায় ডেকে।

ওগো পথিক, আজকে আমার
সকল পরান ব্যেপে
থেকে থেকে হরষ যেন
উঠছে কেঁপে কেঁপে
যেন সময় এসেছে আজ,
ফুরালো মোর যা ছিল কাজ
বাতাস আসে, হে মহারাজ,
তোমার গন্ধ মেখে।

◆ ◆ ◆

I KNOW not from what distant time thou art ever coming nearer to meet me. Thy sun and stars can never keep thee hidden from me for aye.

In many a morning and eve thy footsteps have been heard and thy messenger has come within my heart and called me in secret.

I know not why to-day my life is all astir, and a feeling of tremulous joy is passing through my heart.

It is as if the time were come to wind up my work, and I feel in the air a faint smell of thy sweet presence.

◆ ◆ ◆

Since such a long time ago
You've been coming to meet me.
How can your moon and sun
Hide you.
Through so many ages, morning and evening
Your footsteps ring out,
And in secret a messenger
Has come and called within my heart.

Oh traveler, today
All my being is suffused
With joy now and again
That seems to shiver up within
As though today the time has come,
All my remaining work is done;
The wind comes, oh great king,
Wearing your fragrance.

৪৭ 47

পথ চেয়ে তো কাটল নিশি,
লাগছে মনে ভয়—
সকালবেলা ঘুমিয়ে পড়ি
যদি এমন হয়।
যদি তখন হঠাৎ এসে
দাঁড়ায় আমার দুয়ার-দেশে!
বনচ্ছায়ায় ঘেরা এ ঘর
আছে তো তার জানা—
ওগো, তোরা পথ ছেড়ে দিস,
করিস নে কেউ মানা।

যদি-বা তার পায়ের শব্দে
ঘুম না ভাঙে মোর,
শপথ আমার, তোরা কেহ
ভাঙাস নে সে ঘোর।
চাই নে জাগতে পাখির রবে
নতুন আলোর মহোৎসবে,
চাই নে জাগতে হাওয়ায় আকুল
বকুল ফুলের বাসে—
তোরা আমায় ঘুমোতে দিস
যদিই-বা সে আসে।

ওগো, আমার ঘুম যে ভালো
গভীর অচেতনে—
যদি আমায় জাগায় তারি
আপন পরশনে।
ঘুমের আবেশ যেমনি টুটি
দেখব তারি নয়নদুটি
মুখে আমার তারি হাসি
পড়বে সকৌতুকে—
সে যেন মোর সুখের স্বপন
দাঁড়াবে সম্মুখে।

সে আসবে মোর চোখের 'পরে
সকল আলোর আগে,
তাহারি রূপ মোর প্রভাতের
প্রথম হয়ে জাগে।
প্রথম চমক লাগবে সুখে
চেয়ে তারি করুণ মুখে,
চিত্ত আমার উঠবে কেঁপে
তার চেতনায় ভ'রে—
তোরা আমায় জাগাস নে কেউ,
জাগাবে সেই মোরে।

◆ ◆ ◆

THE night is nearly spent waiting for him in vain. I fear lest in the morning he suddenly come to my door when I have fallen asleep wearied out. Oh friends, leave the way open to him—forbid him not.

If the sound of his steps does not wake me, do not try to rouse me, I pray. I wish not to be called from my sleep by the clamorous choir of birds, by the riot of wind at the festival of morning light. Let me sleep undisturbed even if my lord comes of a sudden to my door.

Ah, my sleep, precious sleep, which only waits for his touch to vanish. Ah, my closed eyes that would open their lids only to the light of his smile when he stands before me like a dream emerging from darkness of sleep.

Let him appear before my sight as the first of all lights and all forms. The first thrill of joy to my awakened soul let it come from his glance. And let my return to myself be immediate return to him.

• • •

The night has passed in watching the road,
        I fear in my mind—
I'll fall asleep in the morning
        And then what if
If he suddenly arrives
And stands at my doorstep!
This house surrounded by forest shadows
        He knows well—
Oh, clear the path for him,
        Don't bar his way.

If the sound of his footsteps
        Doesn't break my sleep,
On my word, none of you, please
        Don't break my doze.
I don't want to wake to birds' sounds
Nor to the grand festival of new light,
I don't want to wake to the bokul flower's fragrance
        Made fervent by the breeze—
Please let me sleep
        Even if he should come.

Oh, my sleep, so restful,
        So deeply unconscious—
If only he wakes me
        With his own touch.
As soon as sleep's daze is broken
I'll see his eyes
On my face, smiling,
        Amused—
As though my dream of happiness
        Stands facing me.

He'll appear in my sight
    Before all other light,
Let his beauty be my dawn's
    First awakening.
My happiness finds its first shine
From looking at his compassionate face,
My soul will tremble
    Filled with knowing him—
Don't wake me, please, none of you,
    It is he who will awaken me.

৪৮ 48

তখন আকাশতলে ঢেউ তুলেছে
পাখিরা গান গেয়ে।
তখন পথের দুটি ধারে
ফুল ফুটেছে ভারে ভারে,
মেঘের কোণে রঙ ধরেছে
দেখি নি কেউ চেয়ে।
মোরা আপন মনে ব্যস্ত হয়ে
চলেছিলেম ধেয়ে।

মোরা সুখের বশে গাই নি তো গান,
করি নি কেউ খেলা।
চাই নি ভুলে ডাহিন-বাঁয়ে,
হাটের লাগি যাই নি গাঁয়ে,
হাসি নি কেউ, কই নি কথা,
করি নি কেউ হেলা।
মোরা ততই বেগে চলেছিলেম
যতই বাড়ে বেলা।

শেষে সূর্য যখন মাঝ-আকাশে,
কপোত ডাকে বনে—
তপ্ত হাওয়ায় ঘুরে ঘুরে
শুকনো পাতা বেড়ায় উড়ে,
বটের তলে রাখালশিশু
ঘুমায় অচেতনে,
আমি জলের ধারে শুলেম এসে
শ্যামল তৃণাসনে।

আমার দলের সবাই আমার পানে
চেয়ে গেল হেসে।
চলে গেল উচ্চশিরে,
চাইল না কেউ পিছু ফিরে,

মিলিয়ে গেল সুদূর ছায়ায়
পথতরুর শেষে।
তারা পেরিয়ে গেল কত যে মাঠ,
কত দূরের দেশে!

ওগো ধন্য তোমরা দুখের যাত্রী,
ধন্য তোমরা সবে।
লাজের ঘায়ে উঠিতে চাই,
মনের মাঝে সাড়া না পাই,
মগ্ন হলেম আনন্দময়
অগাধ অগৌরবে—
পাখির গানে, বাঁশির তানে,
কম্পিত পল্লবে।

আমি মুগ্ধতনু দিলেম মেলে
বসুন্ধরার কোলে।
বাঁশের ছায়া কী কৌতুকে
নাচে আমার চক্ষে মুখে,
আমের মুকুল গন্ধে আমায়
বিধুর ক'রে তোলে—
নয়ন মুদে আসে মৌমাছিদের
গুঞ্জনকল্লোলে।

সেই রৌদ্রে-ঘেরা সবুজ আরাম
মিলিয়ে এল প্রাণে।
ভুলে গেলেম কিসের তরে
বাহির হলেম পথের 'পরে,
ঢেলে দিলেম চেতনা মোর
ছায়ায় গন্ধে গানে—
ধীরে ঘুমিয়ে প'লেম অবশ দেহে
কখন কে তা জানে।

শেষে গভীর ঘুমের মধ্য হতে
ফুটল যখন আঁখি,

চেয়ে দেখি, কখন এসে
দাঁড়িয়ে আছ শিয়রদেশে
তোমার হাসি দিয়ে আমার
অচৈতন্য ঢাকি—
ওগো, ভেবেছিলেম আছে আমার
কত-না পথ বাকি।

মোরা ভেবেছিলেম পরানপণে
সজাগ রব সবে—
সন্ধ্যা হবার আগে যদি
পার হতে না পারি নদী
ভেবেছিলেম তাহা হলেই
সকল ব্যর্থ হবে।
যখন আমি থেমে গেলেম, তুমি
আপনি এলে কবে।

◆ ◆ ◆

The morning sea of silence broke into ripples of bird songs; and the flowers were all merry by the roadside; and the wealth of gold was scattered through the rift of the clouds while we busily went on our way and paid no heed.

We sang no glad songs nor played; we went not to the village for barter; we spoke not a word nor smiled; we lingered not on the way. We quickened our pace more and more as the time sped by.

The sun rose to the mid sky and doves cooed in the shade. Withered leaves danced and whirled in the hot air of noon. The shepherd boy drowsed and dreamed in the shadow of the banyan tree, and I laid myself down by the water and stretched my tired limbs on the grass.

My companions laughed at me in scorn; they

held their heads high and hurried on; they never looked back nor rested; they vanished in the distant blue haze. They crossed many meadows and hills, and passed through strange, far-away countries. All honour to you, heroic host of the interminable path! Mockery and reproach pricked me to rise, but found no response in me. I gave myself up for lost in the depth of a glad humiliation—in the shadow of a dim delight.

The repose of the sun-embroidered green gloom slowly spread over my heart. I forgot for what I had travelled, and I surrendered my mind without struggle to the maze of shadows and songs.

At last, when I woke from my slumber and opened my eyes, I saw thee standing by me, flooding my sleep with thy smile. How I had feared that the path was long and wearisome, and the struggle to reach thee was hard!

◆ ◆ ◆

Then making ripples under the sky
The birds sang their songs.
Then on the two sides of the path
Clusters of flowers blossomed,
Color caught the edge of a cloud
But we didn't stop to look.
We were busy in our minds
And kept going on.

We didn't sing any joyful songs,
No one played.
Didn't look left or right even by mistake,
Didn't go to the village for the market,

Poem 48

No one laughed, no one spoke,
No one forgot their task.
The more the day grew, the faster
We walked.

At last when the sun was mid-sky
And doves called in the wood—
Dried leaves turned and turned
Wandering on the warming air,
Cowherd boys slept unconscious
Under the banyan tree
I lay down at the water's edge
On a green bed of grass.

In my group everyone looked
And laughed at me and went on.
They walked with their heads high,
No one turned to look back,
They merged with distant shadows
Past the wayside trees.
They crossed so many fields,
So many distant lands.

Oh all praise to you wayfarers in misery,
Praise to you all.
With the prick of shame I want to rise,
But my mind doesn't respond,
I am engrossed in the glad
Depths of disgrace—
In birdsong, in flute strains,
In a trembling new leaf.

I spread my enchanted limbs
On the lap of the earth.

The bamboo shadows dance
Curiously over my eyes and face,
The fragrance of mango blossoms
Leaves me overwhelmed—
My eyes droop shut to the hubbub
Of the humming honey bees.

That sunshine-wrapped green ease
Welled into my heart.
I forgot for what purpose
I had set out upon the road,
I poured my wakefulness away
Into the shadows and smells and songs—
I fell slowly asleep, my limbs at ease,
Who knows when.

At last, when my eyes open
Out of the deeps of sleep,
I look and see you there, come sometime
Standing at my head
Covering my unconsciousness
With your smile—
Oh, I had thought I had
Such a long way yet to go.

We had believed with all our hearts
We would all be wakeful—
If before the evening fell
We couldn't cross the river,
We thought if that happened
All would be lost.
When I stopped short, you
Came yourself, who knows when.

৪৯ 49

তব সিংহাসনের আসন হতে
এলে তুমি নেমে—
মোর বিজন ঘরের দ্বারের কাছে
দাঁড়ালে, নাথ, থেমে।
একলা বসে আপন-মনে
গাইতেছিলেম গান,
তোমার কানে গেল সে সুর
এলে তুমি নেমে—
মোর বিজন ঘরের দ্বারের কাছে
দাঁড়ালে, নাথ, থেমে।

তোমার সভায় কত-না গান
কতই আছেন গুণী—
গুণহীনের গানখানি আজ
বাজল তোমার প্রেমে।
লাগল বিশ্বতানের মাঝে
একটি করুণ সুর,
হাতে লয়ে বরণমালা
এলে তুমি নেমে—
মোর বিজন ঘরের দ্বারের কাছে
দাঁড়ালে, নাথ, থেমে।

• • •

YOU came down from your throne and stood at my cottage door.

I was singing all alone in a corner, and the melody caught your ear. You came down and stood at my cottage door.

Masters are many in your hall, and songs are sung there at all hours. But the simple carol of this novice struck at your love. One plaintive little strain mingled with the great music of the world, and with a flower for a prize you came down and stopped at my cottage door.

◆ ◆ ◆

You came down
From the seat of your throne—
And stopped in front of the door
Of my lonely home, and there you stood.
I was sitting alone in my own mind
Singing a song,
That tune reached your ear
And you came down—
And stopped in front of the door
Of my lonely home, and there you stood.

How many songs there are in your hall
And how many gifted singers—
The song of an untalented one
Struck at your love today.
Amid the universe's great melody
It was one plaintive tune,
With a garland in your hand
You came down—
And stopped in front of the door
Of my lonely home, and there you stood.

আমি ভিক্ষা করে ফিরতেছিলেম
গ্রামের পথে পথে,
তুমি তখন চলেছিলে
তোমার স্বর্ণরথে।
অপূর্ব এক স্বপ্ন-সম
লাগতেছিল চক্ষে মম—
কী বিচিত্র শোভা তোমার,
কী বিচিত্র সাজ।
আমি মনে ভাবতেছিলেম,
এ কোন্ মহারাজ।

আজি শুভক্ষণে রাত পোহালো
ভেবেছিলেম তবে,
আজ আমারে দ্বারে দ্বারে
ফিরতে নাহি হবে।
বাহির হতে নাহি হতে
কাহার দেখা পেলেম পথে,
চলিতে রথ ধনধান্য
ছড়াবে দুই ধারে—
মুঠা মুঠা কুড়িয়ে নেব,
নেব ভারে ভারে।

দেখি সহসা রথ থেমে গেল
আমার কাছে এসে,
আমার মুখপানে চেয়ে
নামলে তুমি হেসে।
দেখে মুখের প্রসন্নতা
জুড়িয়ে গেল সকল ব্যথা,
হেনকালে কিসের লাগি
তুমি অকস্মাৎ
'আমায় কিছু দাও গো' বলে
বাড়িয়ে দিলে হাত।

মরি, এ কী কথা রাজাধিরাজ,
'আমায় দাও গো কিছু'!
শুনে ক্ষণকালের তরে
রইনু মাথা-নিচু।
তোমার কী-বা অভাব আছে
ভিখারী ভিক্ষুকের কাছে।
এ কেবল কৌতুকের বশে
আমায় প্রবঞ্চনা।
ঝুলি হতে দিলেম তুলে
একটি ছোটো কণা।

যবে পাত্রখানি ঘরে এনে
উজাড় করি— এ কী!
ভিক্ষামাঝে একটি ছোটো
সোনার কণা দেখি।
দিলেম যা রাজ-ভিখারীরে
স্বর্ণ হয়ে এল ফিরে,
তখন কাঁদি চোখের জলে
দুটি নয়ন ভরে—
তোমায় কেন দিই নি আমার
সকল শূন্য করে।

• • •

I HAD gone a-begging from door to door in the village path, when thy golden chariot appeared in the distance like a gorgeous dream and I wondered who was this King of all kings!

My hopes rose high and methought my evil days were at an end, and I stood waiting for alms to be given unasked and for wealth scattered on all sides in the dust.

The chariot stopped where I stood. Thy glance fell on me and thou camest down with a smile. I felt that the luck of my life had come at last. Then of a sudden thou didst hold out thy right hand and say "What hast thou to give to me?"

Ah, what a kingly jest was it to open thy palm to a beggar to beg! I was confused and stood undecided, and then from my wallet I slowly took out the least little grain of corn and gave it to thee.

But how great my surprise when at the day's end I emptied my bag on the floor to find a least little grain of gold among the poor heap. I bitterly wept and wished that I had had the heart to give thee my all.

◆ ◆ ◆

I had gone begging on the village paths one by one
And was coming back,
And you were riding then
On your golden chariot.
It seemed like a beautiful dream
That appeared before my eyes—
How wondrous your grandeur
How wondrous your attire!
I thought to myself,
What great king is this!

Today in a happy moment my long night is over
I thought then,
Now I won't have to wander
From door to door.
As soon as I stepped out
Whom did I see on the road,

Scattering from his chariot
Wealth on both sides—
I'd gather it up fist by fist
Take it away bag by bag.

I saw the chariot came close to me
And suddenly stop,
Looking at my face
You stepped down smiling.
Seeing your pleased face
All my hurts were healed,
And then suddenly
I don't know why
You said, "Oh, give me something, do,"
And held out your hand.

Oh! what a thing for a king of kings to say,
"Oh, give me something, do"!
I heard it and stood stunned
For a moment, head bowed.
What could you possibly lack
To beg from a beggar himself?
It was only in jest
You misled me this way.
From my satchel I gave you
A small grain of corn.

When I brought home my bag
And emptied it out— what was this!
Among my beggings I saw
A small grain of gold.
What I gave to the royal beggar
Had come back as gold,

Poem 50

And then my eyes filled with tears
    And I cried—
Why didn't I give you everything I had
    Until nothing was left of mine.

তখন রাত্রি আঁধার হল,
সাঙ্গ হল কাজ—
আমরা মনে ভেবেছিলেম
আসবে না কেউ আজ।
মোদের গ্রামে দুয়ার যত
রুদ্ধ হল রাতের মতো,
দু-এক জনে বলেছিল,
'আসবে মহারাজ।'
আমরা হেসে বলেছিলেম,
'আসবে না কেউ আজ।'

দ্বারে যেন আঘাত হল
শুনেছিলেম সবে,
আমরা তখন বলেছিলেম,
'বাতাস বুঝি হবে।'
নিবিয়ে প্রদীপ ঘরে ঘরে
শুয়েছিলেম আলসভরে,
দু-এক জনে বলেছিল,
'দূত এল-বা তবে।'
আমরা হেসে বলেছিলেম,
'বাতাস বুঝি হবে।'

নিশীথরাতে শোনা গেল
কিসের যেন ধ্বনি।
ঘুমের ঘোরে ভেবেছিলেম
মেঘের গরজনি।
ক্ষণে ক্ষণে চেতন করি
কাঁপল ধরা থরহরি,
দু-এক জনে বলেছিল,
'চাকার ঝনঝনি।'
ঘুমের ঘোরে কহি মোরা,
'মেঘের গরজনি।'

Poem 51

তখনো রাত আঁধার আছে,
বেজে উঠল ভেরী,
কে ফুকারে, 'জাগো সবাই,
আর কোরো না দেরি।'
বক্ষ-'পরে দু হাত চেপে
আমরা ভয়ে উঠি কেঁপে,
দু-এক জনে কহে কানে,
'রাজার ধ্বজা হেরি।'
আমরা জেগে উঠে বলি,
'আর তবে নয় দেরি।'

কোথায় আলো, কোথায় মাল্য
কোথায় আয়োজন।
রাজা আমার দেশে এল
কোথায় সিংহাসন।
হায় রে ভাগ্য, হায় রে লজ্জা,
কোথায় সভা, কোথায় সজ্জা!
দু-এক জনে কহে কানে,
'বৃথা এ ক্রন্দন—
রিক্তকরে শূন্যঘরে
করো অভ্যর্থন।'

ওরে, দুয়ার খুলে দে রে,
বাজা, শঙ্খ বাজা!
গভীর রাতে এসেছে আজ
আঁধার ঘরের রাজা।
বজ্র ডাকে শূন্যতলে,
বিদ্যুতেরই ঝিলিক ঝলে,
ছিন্ন শয়ন টেনে এনে
আঙিনা তোর সাজা।
ঝড়ের সাথে হঠাৎ এল
দুঃখরাতের রাজা।

◆ ◆ ◆

THE night darkened. Our day's works had been done. We thought that the last guest had arrived for the night and the doors in the village were all shut. Only some said, The king was to come. We laughed and said "No, it cannot be!"

It seemed there were knocks at the door and we said it was nothing but the wind. We put out the lamps and lay down to sleep. Only some said, "It is the messenger!" We laughed and said "No, it must be the wind!"

There came a sound in the dead of the night. We sleepily thought it was the distant thunder. The earth shook, the walls rocked, and it troubled us in our sleep. Only some said, it was the sound of wheels. We said in a drowsy murmur, "No, it must be the rumbling of clouds!"

The night was still dark when the drum sounded. The voice came "Wake up! delay not!" We pressed our hands on our hearts and shuddered with fear. Some said, "Lo, there is the king's flag!" We stood up on our feet and cried "There is no time for delay!"

The king has come—but where are lights, where are wreaths? Where is the throne to seat him? Oh, shame, Oh utter shame! Where is the hall, the decorations? Someone has said, "Vain is this cry! Greet him with empty hands, lead him into thy rooms all bare!"

Open the doors, let the conch-shells be sounded! In the depth of the night has come the king of our dark, dreary house. The thunder roars in the sky. The darkness shudders with lightning. Bring out thy tattered piece of mat and spread it in the courtyard. With the storm has come of a sudden our king of the fearful night.

◆ ◆ ◆

Then the night grew dark,
And our work was done—
We had thought in our minds
No one would come that day.
All our village doors
Were bolted for the night.
One or two people said,
"The great king will come."
We laughed and said,
"No one will come today."

Something seemed to strike at the door
Which all of us heard,
Then we said,
"It must be the wind."
We put out the lamps in every home
And lay down in lazy rest,
One or two people said,
"Maybe then it's a messenger."
We laughed and said,
"It must be the wind."

In the middle of the night
There came a sound.
In our dazed sleep we thought
It was the rumbling of clouds.

From time to time we felt
The earth tremble and shake,
One or two people said,
"It's the trundling of wheels."
We said in our dazed sleep,
"Rumbling of clouds."

The night was still dark then,
And a drum sounded
Someone called, "Wake up, everyone,
Don't delay any more."
We pressed our hands to our chest
And trembled with fear
One or two people said in our ears,
"I see the king's pennant."
We rose up and said,
"Then there's no time to waste."

Where were the lights, where the garlands,
Where the preparations!
The kind had come to my land
Where was the throne!
Oh ill luck, oh for shame,
Where was the hall, where the decorations!
One or two people said in our ears,
"This crying is useless—
Welcome him with empty hands
into these bare rooms."

Oh, open the doors, do,
Blow the conch-shell, blow!
Today in deepest night
The king of the dark house has come.

Poem 51

The thunder sounds in the emptiness,
Flashes of lightning glitter,
Drag out your tattered mat
    And dress up the courtyard.
Suddenly with the storm has come
    The king of our sorrowful night.

ভেবেছিলাম চেয়ে নেব,
চাই নি সাহস করে—
সন্ধেবেলায় যে মালাটি
গলায় ছিলে পরে—
আমি চাই নি সাহস করে।
ভেবেছিলাম সকাল হলে
যখন পারে যাবে চলে
ছিন্ন মালা শয্যাতলে
রইবে বুঝি পড়ে।
তাই আমি কাঙালের মতো
এসেছিলেম ভোরে—
তবু চাই নি সাহস করে।

এ তো মালা নয় গো, এ যে
তোমার তরবারি।
জ্বলে ওঠে আগুন যেন,
বজ্র-হেন ভারী—
এ যে তোমার তরবারি।
তরুণ আলো জানলা বেয়ে
পড়ল তোমার শয়ন ছেয়ে,
ভোরের পাখি শুধায় গেয়ে
'কী পেলি তুই নারী'।
নয় এ মালা, নয় এ থালা,
গন্ধজলের ঝারি,
এ যে ভীষণ তরবারি।

তাই তো আমি ভাবি বসে
এ কী তোমার দান।
কোথায় এরে লুকিয়ে রাখি
নাই যে হেন স্থান।
ওগো, এ কী তোমার দান।

Poem 52

শক্তিহীনা মরি লাজে,
এ ভূষণ কি আমায় সাজে।
রাখতে গেলে বুকের মাঝে
ব্যথা যে পায় প্রাণ।
তবু আমি বইব বুকে
এই বেদনার মান—
নিয়ে তোমারি এই দান।

আজকে হতে জগৎমাঝে
ছাড়ব আমি ভয়,
আজ হতে মোর সকল কাজে
তোমার হবে জয়—
আমি ছাড়ব সকল ভয়।
মরণকে মোর দোসর করে
রেখে গেছ আমার ঘরে,
আমি তারে বরণ ক'রে
রাখব পরান-ময়।
তোমার তরবারি আমার
করবে বাঁধন ক্ষয়।
আমি ছাড়ব সকল ভয়।

তোমার লাগি অঙ্গ ভরি
করব না আর সাজ।
নাই-বা তুমি ফিরে এলে
ওগো হৃদয়রাজ।
আমি করব না আর সাজ।
ধুলায় বসে তোমার তরে
কাঁদব না আর একলা ঘরে,
তোমার লাগি ঘরে-পরে
মানব না আর লাজ।
তোমার তরবারি আমায়
সাজিয়ে দিল আজ,
আমি করব না আর সাজ।

◆ ◆ ◆

I THOUGHT I should ask of thee—but I dared not—the rose wreath thou hadst on thy neck. Thus I waited for the morning, when thou didst depart, to find a few fragments on the bed. And like a beggar I searched in the dawn only for a stray petal or two.

Ah me, what is it I find? What token left of thy love? It is no flower, no spices, no vase of perfumed water. It is thy mighty sword, flashing as a flame, heavy as a bolt of thunder. The young light of morning comes through the window and spreads itself upon thy bed. The morning bird twitters and asks, "Woman, what hast thou got?" No, it is no flower, nor spices, nor vase of perfumed water—it is thy dreadful sword.

I sit and muse in wonder, what gift is this of thine. I can find no place where to hide it. I am ashamed to wear it, frail as I am, and it hurts me when I press it to my bosom. Yet shall I bear in my heart this honour of the burden of pain, this gift of thine.

From now there shall be no fear left for me in this world, and thou shalt be victorious in all my strife. Thou hast left death for my companion and I shall crown him with my life. Thy sword is with me to cut asunder my bonds, and there shall be no fear left for me in the world.

From now I leave off all petty decorations. Lord of my heart, no more shall there be for me waiting and weeping in corners, no more shy and soft demeanour. Thou hast given me thy sword for adornment. No more doll's decorations for me!

• • •

I thought I'd ask for it
    But I didn't dare to ask—
The garland you wore on your neck
    In the evening—
I   didn't dare to ask.
I thought when you left
In the morning
I'd find the torn garland
    On the bed.
So I came like a beggar
    In the dawn—
Still   I didn't dare to ask.

But oh, this isn't a garland,
    This is your mighty sword.
It flashes like fire,
    Heavy as a thunderbolt—
This is   your mighty sword.
The young light of morning climbs
Through the window, spreads across your bed,
Dawn's bird, singing, asks
    "Woman, what did you get?"
This isn't a garland, nor a platter,
    Not a jar of perfumed water,
This   is a terrible sword.

That's why I sit and wonder
    What kind of gift is this?
Where can I hide it
    There's no place I find.
Oh,   what kind of gift is this?

Powerless, I'm full of shame
Does this ornament suit me!
If I try to press it to my chest
It's an ache in my heart.
Still, I'll bear it on my chest,
The honor of this pain—
Taking this your gift to me.

From today I'll shed all fear
In this world,
From today in all my tasks
Victory will be yours—
I'll shed all fear today.
You've made death my companion
And left it in my home
I'll welcome it
And keep it with my life.
Your sword
Will cut through my bonds.
I'll shed all fear today.

No longer will I
Adorn my limbs for you.
Nor when you return
Oh king of my heart
Will I adorn any more
I won't sit in the dust and wait for you
Won't cry alone in my room any more,
I won't be bashful any more
With anyone for your sake.
Your sword
Adorns me today,
I won't adorn myself any more.

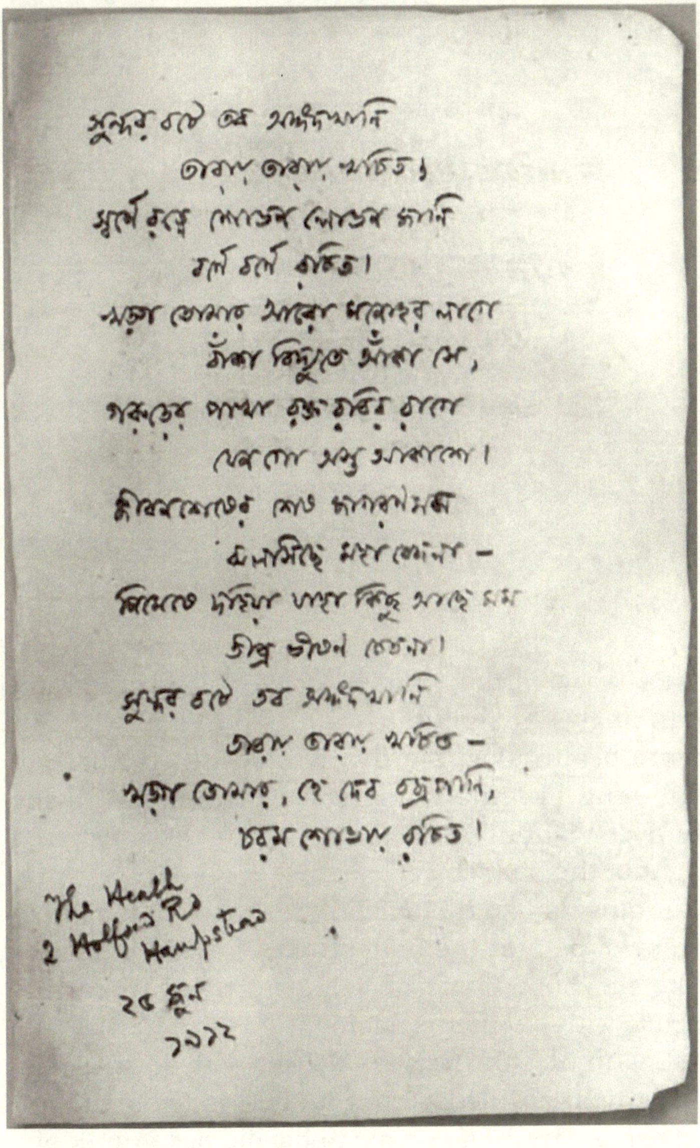

সুন্দর বটে তব অঙ্গদখানি
তারায় তারায় খচিত।
স্বর্ণে রত্নে শোভন লোভন জানি
বর্ণে বর্ণে রচিত।
খড়্গ তোমার আরো মনোহর লাগে
বাঁকা বিদ্যুতে আঁকা সে,
গরুড়ের পাখা রক্ত রবির রাগে
যেন গো অস্ত আকাশে।
জীবনশেষের শেষ জাগরণসম
ঝলসিছে মহাবেদনা —
নিমেষে দহিয়া যাহা কিছু আছে মম
তীব্র ভীষণ চেতনা।
সুন্দর বটে তব অঙ্গদখানি
তারায় তারায় খচিত —
খড়্গ তোমার, হে দেব বজ্রপাণি,
চরম শোভায় রচিত।

The Heath
2 Holford Rd
Hampstead

২৮ জুন
১৯১২

সুন্দর বটে তব অঙ্গদখানি
তারায় তারায় খচিত,
স্বর্ণে রত্নে শোভন লোভন জানি
বর্ণে বর্ণে রচিত।
খড়্গ তোমার আরো মনোহর লাগে
বাঁকা বিদ্যুতে আঁকা সে,
গরুড়ের পাখা রক্তরবির রাগে
যেন গো অস্ত-আকাশে।
জীবন-শেষের শেষ জাগরণসম
ঝলসিছে মহাবেদনা—
নিমেষে দহিয়া যাহা-কিছু আছে মম
তীব্র ভীষণ চেতনা।
সুন্দর বটে তব অঙ্গদখানি
তারায় তারায় খচিত—
খড়্গ তোমার, হে দেব বজ্রপাণি,
চরম শোভায় রচিত।

• • •

Beautiful is thy wristlet, decked with stars and cunningly wrought in myriad-coloured jewels. But more beautiful to me thy sword with its curve of lightning like the outspread wings of the divine bird of Vishnu, perfectly poised in the angry red light of the sunset.

It quivers like the one last response of life in ecstasy of pain at the final stroke of death; it shines like the pure flame of being burning up earthly sense with one fierce flash.

Beautiful is thy wristlet, decked with starry gems; but thy sword, O lord of thunder, is wrought with uttermost beauty, terrible to behold or to think of.

◆ ◆ ◆

Truly, it's beautiful, your bracelet,
        Chased with star upon star,
Crafted with gems and gold, color piled on color
        Graceful and tempting, I know.
Your sword is even more delightful to me
        For its etched jagged lightning,
Like the wings of the divine Gorur spread
        On the angry blood of the sunset sky.
Like the last flicker at life's end
        A great pain flashes—
Burning in an instant whatever's mine,
        A sharp, terrible awareness.
Truly, it's beautiful, your bracelet,
        Chased with star upon star—
But your sword, o lord, bearer of thunder,
        Is crafted with utmost grace.

তোমার কাছে চাই নি কিছু,
জানাই নি মোর নাম—
তুমি যখন বিদায় নিলে
নীরব রহিলাম।
একলা ছিলেম কুয়ার ধারে
নিমের ছায়াতলে,
কলস নিয়ে সবাই তখন
পাড়ায় গেছে চলে।
আমায় তারা ডেকে গেল,
'আয় গো, বেলা যায়।'
কোন্ আলসে রইনু বসে
কিসের ভাবনায়!

পদধ্বনি শুনি নাইকো
কখন তুমি এলে।
কইলে কথা ক্লান্তকণ্ঠে
করুণ চক্ষু মেলে—
'তৃষাকাতর পান্থ আমি'—
শুনে চমকে উঠে
জলের ধারা দিলেম ঢেলে
তোমার করপুটে।
মর্মরিয়া কাঁপে পাতা,
কোকিল কোথা ডাকে,
বাবলা ফুলের গন্ধ ওঠে
পল্লীপথের বাঁকে।

যখন তুমি শুধালে নাম
পেলেম বড়ো লাজ
তোমার মনে থাকার মতো
করেছি কোন্ কাজ।
তোমায় দিতে পেরেছিলেম
একটু তৃষার জল,

এই কথাটি আমার মনে
রহিল সম্বল।
কুয়ার ধারে দুপুরবেলা
তেমনি ডাকে পাখি,
তেমনি কাঁপে নিমের পাতা—
আমি বসেই থাকি।

◆ ◆ ◆

I ASKED nothing from thee; I uttered not my name to thine ear. When thou took'st thy leave I stood silent. I was alone by the well where the shadow of the tree fell aslant, and the women had gone home with their brown earthen pitchers full to the brim. They called me and shouted, "Come with us, the morning is wearing on to noon." But I languidly lingered awhile lost in the midst of vague musings.

I heard not thy steps as thou camest. Thine eyes were sad when they fell on me; thy voice was tired as thou spokest low—"Ah, I am a thirsty traveller." I started up from my daydreams and poured water from my jar on thy joined palms. The leaves rustled overhead; the cuckoo sang from the unseen dark, and perfume of *babla* flowers came from the bend of the road.

I stood speechless with shame when my name thou didst ask. Indeed, what had I done for thee to keep me in remembrance? But the memory that I could give water to thee to allay thy thirst will cling to my heart and enfold it in sweetness. The morning hour is late, the bird sings in weary notes, neem leaves rustle overhead and I sit and think and think.

• • •

I didn't ask you for anything,
        Didn't tell you my name—
When you took your leave
        I stayed silent.
I was alone beside the well
        In the shade of the neem,
Everyone had gone home by then
        Carrying their pitchers.
They called to me as they went,
        "Come now, the morning passes by."
In what lassitude I stayed seated
        Thinking of I don't know what!

I didn't hear your footsteps
        Or when you came.
You spoke in a tired voice
        Sadness in your eyes—
"I'm a traveler aching with thirst"—
        Hearing this, I started
And poured a stream of water
        Into your cupped hands.
The leaves rustle and shiver,
        Somewhere the cuckoo calls,
The fragrance of babla flowers
        Rises from the bend of the village path.

When you asked my name
        I was much ashamed,
What had I done
        That you would remember?
I was able to give you
        A little water for your thirst,

Poem 54

This memory will stay
        A treasure in my heart.
In the afternoon beside the well
        The birds call the same way,
The same way, the neem leaves shiver—
        And I sit there still.

৫৫ 55

এখনো ঘোর ভাঙে না তোর যে
মেলে না তোর আঁখি,
কাঁটার বনে ফুল ফুটেছে রে
জানিস নে তুই তা কি।
ওরে অলস, জানিস নে তুই তা কি।
জাগো এবার জাগো,
বেলা কাটাস না গো।

কঠিন পথের শেষে
কোথায় অগম বিজন দেশে
ও সেই বন্ধু আমার একলা আছে গো,
দিস নে তারে ফাঁকি।
চিরজীবন দিস নে তারে ফাঁকি।
জাগো এবার জাগো,
বেলা কাটাস না গো।

প্রখর রবির তাপে
নাহয় শুষ্ক গগন কাঁপে,
নাহয় দগ্ধ বালু তপ্ত আঁচলে
দিক চারি দিক ঢাকি।
পিপাসাতে দিক চারি দিক ঢাকি

মনের মাঝে চাহি
দেখ্ রে আনন্দ কি নাহি।
পথে পায়ে পায়ে দুখের বাঁশরি
বাজবে তোরে ডাকি।
মধুর সুরে বাজবে তোরে ডাকি।
জাগো এবার জাগো,
বেলা কাটাস না গো।

• • •

LANGUOR is upon your heart and the slumber is still on your eyes.

Has not the word come to you that the flower is reigning in splendour among thorns? Wake, oh awaken! Let not the time pass in vain!

At the end of the stony path, in the country of virgin solitude my friend is sitting all alone. Deceive him not. Wake, oh awaken!

What if the sky pants and trembles with the heat of the midday sun—what if the burning sand spreads its mantle of thirst—

Is there no joy in the deep of your heart? At every footfall of yours, will not the harp of the road break out in sweet music of pain?

◆ ◆ ◆

Your lassitude is still not broken
Your eyes aren't open yet,
In the forest of thorns the flowers have bloomed, oh
How could you not know.
Oh lazy man, how could you not know.
Awake now awake,
Oh don't let the morning go.

At the end of a difficult path
Somewhere in an unreachable, unpeopled land
Oh that friend of mine is alone, oh
Don't deceive him now.
In all your life don't deceive him now.
Awake now awake,
Oh don't let the morning go.

In the severe heat of the sun
Even if the dried-out sky trembles,
Even if scorched sand covers the heated land
In every direction.
Thirst covers every direction.

Look within your heart
And see, is there no joy?
Step after step on the road, the flute of sadness
Will play and call out to you.
Sweet melodies will play and call out to you.
Awake now awake,
Oh don't let the morning go.

৫৬ 56

তাই তোমার আনন্দ আমার 'পর
তুমি তাই এসেছ নীচে।
আমায় নইলে, ত্রিভুবনেশ্বর,
তোমার প্রেম হত যে মিছে।
আমায় নিয়ে মেলেছ এই মেলা,
আমার হিয়ায় চলছে রসের খেলা,
মোর জীবনে বিচিত্ররূপ ধ'রে
তোমার ইচ্ছা তরঙ্গিছে।

তাই তো তুমি রাজার রাজা হয়ে
তবু আমার হৃদয় লাগি
ফিরছ কত মনোহরণ-বেশে
প্রভু নিত্য আছ জাগি।
তাই তো, প্রভু, হেথায় এল নেমে,
তোমারি প্রেম ভক্ত প্রাণের প্রেমে,
মূর্তি তোমার যুগলসম্মিলনে
সেথায় পূর্ণ প্রকাশিছে।

• • •

THUS it is that thy joy in me is so full. Thus it is that thou hast come down to me. O thou lord of all heavens, where would be thy love if I were not?

Thou hast taken me as thy partner of all this wealth. In my heart is the endless play of thy delight. In my life thy will is ever taking shape.

And for this, thou who art the King of kings hast decked thyself in beauty to captivate my heart. And for this thy love loses itself in the love of thy lover, and there art thou seen in the perfect union of two.

• • •

That's why your joy is upon me
That's why you've come down.
Or else, oh lord of the three worlds,
Your love would be a lie to me.
You've taken me and spread out this fair,
Delight plays on in my heart,
Your wish takes wonderful shape
And billows through my life.

That's why, though you are the king of kings
Still you're ready always
To return in so many enchanting forms,
Lord, for the sake of my heart.
That's why, lord, your love came down here,
In love with a devoted life,
And there your form is fully seen
In the perfect union of the two.

৫৭ 57

আলো, আমার আলো, ওগো
আলো ভুবনভরা।
আলো নয়ন-ধোওয়া আমার
আলো হৃদয়হরা।
নাচে আলো নাচে— ও ভাই
আমার প্রাণের কাছে,
বাজে আলো বাজে— ও ভাই
হৃদয়-বীণার মাঝে;
জাগে আকাশ ছোটে বাতাস
হাসে সকল ধরা।
আলো, আমার আলো, ওগো
আলো ভুবনভরা।
আলোর স্রোতে পাল তুলেছে
হাজার প্রজাপতি।
আলোর ঢেউয়ে উঠল নেচে
মল্লিকা মালতী।
মেঘে মেঘে সোনা— ও ভাই
যায় না মানিক গোনা,
পাতায় পাতায় হাসি— ও ভাই
পুলক রাশি রাশি,
সুরনদীর কূল ডুবেছে
সুধা-নিঝর-ঝরা।
আলো, আমার আলো, ওগো
আলো ভুবনভরা।

• • •

LIGHT, my light, the world-filling light, the eye-kissing light, heart-sweetening light!

Ah, the light dances, my darling, at the centre of my life; the light strikes, my darling, the chords of my love; the sky opens, the wind runs wild, laughter passes over the earth.

The butterflies spread their sails on the sea of light. Lilies and jasmines surge up on the crest of the waves of light.

The light is shattered into gold on every cloud, my darling, and it scatters gems in profusion.

Mirth spreads from leaf to leaf, my darling, and gladness without measure. The heaven's river has drowned its banks and the flood of joy is abroad.

◆ ◆ ◆

Light of mine, oh, this light,
Light filling the skies.
Washing over my eyes this light
Light stealing my heart.
Dances the light dances— oh my friend,
At my life's core,
Plays the light plays— oh my brother,
The strings of my heart;
The sky wakes the wind runs
All the world laughs.
Light of mine, oh this light,
Light filling the skies.
A thousand butterflies spread their sails
On the stream of light.
Jasmine flowers rise up dancing
On the waves of light.
Gold in every cloud— my brother,
Gems beyond count,
Laughter in every leaf— my friend,
Delight unbound,

Poem 57

Heaven's river's banks are drowned
        Endless nectar flows.
Light of mine, oh, this light,
        Light filling the skies.

৫৮ 58

যেন শেষ গানে মোর সব রাগিণী পূরে–
আমার সব আনন্দ মেলে তাহার সুরে।
যে আনন্দে মাটির ধরা হাসে
অধীর হয়ে তরুলতায় ঘাসে,
যে আনন্দে দুই পাগলের মতো
জীবন-মরণ বেড়ায় ভুবন ঘুরে–
সেই আনন্দ মেলে তাহার সুরে।

যে আনন্দ আসে ঝড়ের বেশে,
ঘুমন্ত প্রাণ জাগায় অট্ট হেসে।
যে আনন্দ দাঁড়ায় আঁখিজলে
দুঃখ-ব্যথার রক্তশতদলে,
যা আছে সব ধুলায় ফেলে দিয়ে
যে আনন্দে বচন নাহি ফুরে–
সেই আনন্দ মেলে তাহার সুরে।

• • •

LET all the strains of joy mingle in my last song—the joy that makes the earth flow over in the riotous excess of the grass, the joy that sets the twin brothers, life and death, dancing over the wide world, the joy that sweeps in with the tempest, shaking and waking all life with laughter, the joy that sits still with its tears on the open red lotus of pain, and the joy that throws everything it has upon the dust, and knows not a word.

• • •

Poem 58

Let all my melodies fill my last song—
All my joys blend into his tune.
    The earthen world's joy as it grows eager
    And laughs in its trees and plants and grass,
    The joy with which life and death
        Like two madmen wander the universe—
        Those joys blend into his tune.

The joy that comes in the shape of a storm,
Awakens sleeping lives with its roaring laugh.
    The joy that stands in welling tears
    In the blood lotus of grief and pain,
    That casts everything into the dust
        The joy in which eloquence never ends—
        Those joys blend into his tune.

৫৯ 59

এই তো তোমার প্রেম, ওগো
হৃদয়হরণ।
এই-যে পাতায় আলো নাচে
সোনার বরন।
এই-যে মধুর আলসভরে
মেঘ ভেসে যায় আকাশ-'পরে,
এই-যে বাতাস দেহে করে
অমৃত ক্ষরণ।
এই তো তোমার প্রেম, ওগো
হৃদয়হরণ।

প্রভাত-আলোর ধারায় আমার
নয়ন ভেসেছে।
এই তোমারি প্রেমের বাণী
প্রাণে এসেছে।
তোমারি মুখ ওই নুয়েছে,
মুখে আমার চোখ থুয়েছে,
আমার হৃদয় আজ ছুঁয়েছে
তোমারি চরণ।

◆ ◆ ◆

YES, I know, this is nothing but thy love, O beloved of my heart—this golden light that dances upon the leaves, these idle clouds sailing across the sky, this passing breeze leaving its coolness upon my forehead.

The morning light has flooded my eyes—this is thy message to my heart. Thy face is bent from above, thy eyes look down on my eyes, and my heart has touched thy feet.

◆ ◆ ◆

This is what your love is, oh my
Heart-robber.
This light that dances in the leaves
The color of gold.
These clouds, full of a sweet lassitude
Floating away in the sky,
This breeze that brushes my skin
With its nectar fragrance.
This is what your love is, oh my
Heart-robber.

On the stream of dawn-light
My gaze floats away.
This, your own voice of love,
Enters my life.
It's your face that leans down thus,
You rest your eyes on my face,
And today my heart touches
Your feet.

৬০ 60

জগৎ-পারাবারের তীরে
ছেলেরা করে মেলা।
অন্তহীন গগনতল
মাথার 'পরে অচঞ্চল,
ফেনিল ওই সুনীল জল
নাচিছে সারা বেলা।
উঠিছে তটে কী কোলাহল—
ছেলেরা করে মেলা।

বালুকা দিয়ে বাঁধিছে ঘর,
ঝিনুক নিয়ে খেলা।
বিপুল নীল সলিল-'পরি
ভাসায় তারা খেলার তরী
আপন হাতে হেলায় গড়ি
পাতায়-গাঁথা ভেলা।
জগৎ-পারাবারের তীরে
ছেলেরা করে খেলা।

জানে না তারা সাঁতার দেওয়া,
জানে না জাল ফেলা।
ডুবারি ডুবে মুকুতা চেয়ে,
বণিক ধায় তরণী বেয়ে,
ছেলেরা নুড়ি কুড়ায়ে পেয়ে
সাজায় বসি ঢেলা।
রতন ধন খোঁজে না তারা,
জানে না জাল ফেলা।

ফেনিয়ে উঠে সাগর হাসে,
হাসে সাগর-বেলা।
ভীষণ ঢেউ শিশুর কানে
রচিছে গাথা তরল তানে,

দোলনা ধরি যেমন গানে
জননী দেয় ঠেলা।
সাগর খেলে শিশুর সাথে,
হাসে সাগর-বেলা।

জগৎ-পারাবারের তীরে
ছেলেরা করে মেলা।
ঝঞ্ঝা ফিরে গগনতলে,
তরণী ডুবে সুদূর জলে,
মরণ-দূত উড়িয়া চলে,
ছেলেরা করে খেলা।
জগৎ-পারাবারের তীরে
শিশুর মহামেলা।

◆ ◆ ◆

On the seashore of endless worlds children meet. The infinite sky is motionless overhead and the restless water is boisterous. On the seashore of endless worlds the children meet with shouts and dances.

They build their houses with sand and they play with empty shells. With withered leaves they weave their boats and smilingly float them on the vast deep. Children have their play on the seashore of worlds.

They know not how to swim, they know not how to cast nets. Pearl fishers dive for pearls, merchants sail in their ships, while children gather pebbles and scatter them again. They seek not for hidden treasures, they know not how to cast nets.

The sea surges up with laughter and pale gleams the smile of the sea beach. Death-dealing waves sing meaningless ballads to the children, even like a mother while rocking her baby's cradle. The sea plays with children, and pale gleams the smile of the sea beach.

On the seashore of endless worlds children meet. Tempest roams in the pathless sky, ships get wrecked in the trackless water, death is abroad and children play. On the seashore of endless worlds is the great meeting of children.

◆ ◆ ◆

On the world's ocean-shore
        Boys meet and revel.
Beneath the endless sky
Motionless overhead,
That frothing, deep-blue water
        Dances all day.
What a tumult rises on the shore—
        Boys meet and revel.

They build houses with sand,
        Play with seashells.
On the vast blue water
They float their play-boats
They stitch with leaves themselves
        Push off their rafts aslant.
On the world's ocean-shore
        Boys play their games.

They don't know how to swim
        Don't know how to cast a net.
The diver dives wanting a pearl,
The merchant sails his ship with speed,

Poem 60

The boys find pebbles and pick them up
        And set them out in heaps.
They don't search for gems or wealth,
        Don't know how to cast a net.

The ocean froths up, laughing,
        The seashore smiles.
The terrible waves make liquid melodies
In the children's ears,
Songs like a mother sings
        As she pushes the cradle.
The ocean plays with the children,
        The seashore smiles.

On the world's ocean-shore,
        Boys meet and revel.
A storm wanders beneath the sky,
A ship sinks in distant waters,
Death's messenger flies about,
        And boys play their games.
On the world's ocean-shore
        A grand meeting of children.

খোকার চোখে যে ঘুম আসে
সকল-তাপ-নাশা—
জান কি কেউ কোথা হতে যে
করে সে যাওয়া-আসা।
শুনেছি রূপকথার গাঁয়ে
জোনাকি-জ্বলা বনের ছায়ে
দুলিছে দুটি পারুল-কুঁড়ি,
তাহারি মাঝে বাসা—
সেখান থেকে খোকার চোখে
করে সে যাওয়া-আসা।

খোকার ঠোঁটে যে হাসিখানি
চমকে ঘুমঘোরে—
কোন্ দেশে যে জনম তার
কে কবে তাহা মোরে।
শুনেছি কোন্ শরৎ-মেঘে
শিশু-শশীর কিরণ লেগে
সে হাসিরুচি জনমি ছিল
শিশিরশুচি ভোরে—
খোকার ঠোঁটে যে হাসিখানি
চমকে ঘুমঘোরে।

খোকার গায়ে মিলিয়ে আছে
যে কচি কোমলতা—
জান কি সে যে এতটা কাল
লুকিয়ে ছিল কোথা।
মা যবে ছিল কিশোরী মেয়ে
করুণ তারি পরান ছেয়ে
মাধুরীরূপে মুরছি ছিল
কহে নি কোনো কথা—
খোকার গায়ে মিলিয়ে আছে
যে কচি কোমলতা।

[আশিস আসি পরশ করে
খোকারে ঘিরে ঘিরে—
জান কি কেহ কোথা হতে সে
বরষে তার শিরে।
ফাগুনে নব মলয়শ্বাসে,
শ্রাবণে নব নীপের বাসে,
আশিনে নব ধান্যদলে,
আষাঢ়ে নব নীরে—
আশিস আসি পরশ করে
খোকারে ঘিরে ঘিরে।

এই-যে খোকা তরুণতনু
নতুন মেলে আঁখি—
ইহার ভার কে লবে আজি
তোমরা জান তা কি।
হিরণময় কিরণ-ঝোলা
যাঁহার এই ভুবন-দোলা
তপন-শশী-তারার কোলে
দেবেন এরে রাখি—
এই-যে খোকা তরুণতনু
নতুন মেলে আঁখি।]

◆ ◆ ◆

THE sleep that flits on baby's eyes—does anybody know from where it comes? Yes, there is a rumour that it has its dwelling where, in the fairy village among shadows of the forest dimly lit with glow-worms, there hang two timid buds of enchantment. From there it comes to kiss baby's eyes.

The smile that flickers on baby's lips when he sleeps—does anybody know where it was born? Yes, there is a rumour that a young pale beam of a crescent moon touched the edge of a vanishing autumn cloud, and there the smile was first born in the dream of a dew-washed morning—the smile that flickers on baby's lips when he sleeps.

The sweet, soft freshness that blooms on baby's limbs—does anybody know where it was hidden so long? Yes, when the mother was a young girl it lay pervading her heart in tender and silent mystery of love—the sweet, soft freshness that has bloomed on baby's limbs.*

◆ ◆ ◆

The sleep that comes to an infant's eyes
Ending every unhappiness—
Do any of you know from where
It comes and where it goes.
I've heard in a fairytale village
In the shadows of a forest lit by fireflies
There sway two trumpet-flower buds,
Among them is its home—
From there to the infant's eyes
It comes and there it goes.

The smile on an infant's lips
That flashes in unconscious sleep—
In which land was it born
Who will tell me that.
I've heard an autumn cloud
Was brushed by a baby moon's gleam
And that smile-glow was born
On a dawn of the purest dew—
The smile on an infant's lips
That flashes in unconscious sleep.

* Rabindranath chooses not to translate the last two stanzas of the original; I have included them in my translation.

That delicate tenderness that's
        In an infant's limbs—
Do you know where it hid
        For such a long time.
When the mother was a young girl
It spread through her tender heart
And lay in silent sweetness
        It didn't say a word—
That delicate tenderness that's
        In an infant's limbs.

A benediction surrounds
        And touches the infant—
Do any of you know from where it comes
        And showers upon the infant's head.
From the new breath of a cool springtime,
From a new kadamba-flower's scent in the rain,
From a new blade of paddy in the autumn,
        From the rainfall of a new monsoon—
A benediction surrounds
        And touches the infant.

This infant with its young limbs
        Newly opening its eyes—
Who will now take this task
        Do you all know.
The one whose universe-cradle
Swings from golden rays
In the lap of sun-moon-stars
        He will keep this infant—
This infant with its young limbs
        Just newly opening its eyes.

৬২ 62

রঙিন খেলেনা দিলে ও রাঙা হাতে
তখন বুঝি রে বাছা, কেন যে প্রাতে
এত রঙ খেলে মেঘে, জলে রঙ ওঠে জেগে,
কেন এত রঙ লেগে ফুলের পাতে—
রাঙা খেলা দেখি যবে ও রাঙা হাতে।

গান গেয়ে তোরে আমি নাচাই যবে
আপন হৃদয়-মাঝে বুঝি রে তবে,
পাতায় পাতায় বনে ধ্বনি এত কী কারণে,
ঢেউ বহে নিজমনে তরল রবে,
বুঝি তা তোমারে গান শুনাই যবে।

যখন নবনী দিই লোলুপ করে
হাতে মুখে মেখেচুকে বেড়াও ঘরে,
তখন বুঝিতে পারি স্বাদু কেন নদীবারি,
ফল মধুরসে ভারী কিসের তরে,
যখন নবনী দিই লোলুপ করে।

যখন চুমিয়ে তোর বদনখানি
হাসিটি ফুটায়ে তুলি তখনি জানি
আকাশ কিসের সুখে আলো দেয় মোর মুখে,
বায়ু দিয়ে যায় বুকে অমৃত আনি—
বুঝি তা চুমিলে তোর বদনখানি।

◆ ◆ ◆

WHEN I bring to you coloured toys, my child, I understand why there is such a play of colours on clouds, on water, and why flowers are painted in tints—when I give coloured toys to you, my child.

When I sing to make you dance I truly know why there is music in leaves, and why waves send their chorus of voices to the heart of the listening earth—when I sing to make you dance.

When I bring sweet things to your greedy hands I know why there is honey in the cup of the flower and why fruits are secretly filled with sweet juice—when I bring sweet things to your greedy hands.

When I kiss your face to make you smile, my darling, I surely understand what the pleasure is that streams from the sky in morning light, and what delight that is which the summer breeze brings to my body—when I kiss you to make you smile.

◆ ◆ ◆

When I give colored toys for those fair hands
Then I understand, child of mine, why at dawn
So many colors play on the clouds, colors rise up on the water,
Why so many colors touch the flowers—
When I see the colors play in those fair hands.

When I sing and make you dance
Then I understand within my heart,
Why from leaf to leaf there is such music in the forest,
The waves flow on, absorbed in their liquid sound,
I understand that when I sing you a song.

When I give sweet cream into your greedy hands
You smear your hands and face and wander the house,
Then I can understand why riverwater is sweet,
Why a fruit is heavy with honeyed juice,
When I give sweet cream into your greedy hands.

When I kiss that face of yours
And make that smile bloom, right then I know
For what pleasure the sky gives light to my face,
And the breeze carries nectar in its heart to give to me—
This I understand when I kiss that face of yours.

৬৩ 63

কত অজানারে জানাইলে তুমি,
কত ঘরে দিলে ঠাঁই—
দূরকে করিলে নিকট, বন্ধু,
পরকে করিলে ভাই।
পুরানো আবাস ছেড়ে যাই তবে
মনে ভেবে মরি কী জানি কী হবে,
নূতনের মাঝে তুমি পুরাতন,
সে কথা যে ভুলে যাই।
দূরকে করিলে নিকট, বন্ধু,
পরকে করিলে ভাই।

জীবনে মরণে নিখিল ভুবনে
যখনি যেখানে লবে,
চিরজনমের পরিচিত ওহে,
তুমিই চিনাবে সবে।
তোমারে জানিলে নাহি কেহ পর,
নাহি কোনো মানা, নাহি কোনো ডর;
সবারে মিলায়ে তুমি জাগিতেছ,
দেখা যেন সদা পাই।
দূরকে করিলে নিকট, বন্ধু,
পরকে করিলে ভাই।

◆ ◆ ◆

THOU hast made me known to friends whom I knew not. Thou hast given me seats in homes not my own. Thou hast brought the distant near and made a brother of the stranger.

I am uneasy at heart when I have to leave my accustomed shelter; I forget that there abides the old in the new, and that there also thou abidest.

Through birth and death, in this world or in others,

wherever thou leadest me it is thou, the same, the one companion of my endless life who ever linkest my heart with bonds of joy to the unfamiliar.

When one knows thee, then alien there is none, then no door is shut. Oh, grant me my prayer that I may never lose the bliss of the touch of the one in the play of the many.*

◆ ◆ ◆

How many unknown people you've made known,
In how many homes given me a place—
You've made the distant near, my friend,
Made the stranger a brother.
When I have to leave my old abode
I die inside to think what may happen,
I forget that among the new
You are the old and familiar.
You've made the distant near, my friend,
Made the stranger a brother.

In life and death across the whole universe
Whenever wherever you take me,
Oh, my lifelong familiar,
It's you who will make everyone known.
Knowing you means no one's a stranger
Nothing's closed off, there's no fear,
You rise among the many you make one;
May I see you always.
You've made the distant near, my friend,
Made the stranger a brother.

* The last part of this sentence ("the bliss . . . of the many") is a superb addition by Rabindranath that does not exist in the original.

৬৪ 64

কাশের বনে শূন্য নদীর তীরে
আমি তারে জিজ্ঞাসিলাম ডেকে,
‘একলা পথে কে তুমি যাও ধীরে
আঁচল-আড়ে প্রদীপখানি ঢেকে।
আমার ঘরে হয় নি আলো জ্বালা,
দেউটি তব হেথায় রাখো বালা।’
গোধূলিতে দুটি নয়ন কালো
ক্ষণেক-তরে আমার মুখে তুলে
সে কহিল, ‘ভাসিয়ে দেব আলো,
দিনের শেষে তাই এসেছি কূলে।’
চেয়ে দেখি দাঁড়িয়ে কাশের বনে,
প্রদীপ ভেসে গেল অকারণে।

ভরা সাঁঝে আঁধার হয়ে এলে
আমি ডেকে জিজ্ঞাসিলাম তারে,
‘তোমার ঘরে সকল আলো জ্বেলে
এ দীপখানি সঁপিতে যাও কারে।
আমার ঘরে হয় নি আলো জ্বালা,
দেউটি তব হেথায় রাখো বালা।’
আমার মুখে দুটি নয়ন কালো
ক্ষণেক-তরে রইল চেয়ে ভুলে।
সে কহিল, ‘আমার এ যে আলো
আকাশপ্রদীপ শূন্যে দিব তুলে।’
চেয়ে দেখি শূন্য গগনকোণে
প্রদীপখানি জ্বলে অকারণে।

অমাবস্যা আঁধার দুই-পহরে
জিজ্ঞাসিলাম তাহার কাছে গিয়ে,
‘ওগো, তুমি চলেছ কার তরে
প্রদীপখানি বুকের কাছে নিয়ে।
আমার ঘরে হয় নি আলো জ্বালা,
দেউটি তব হেথায় রাখো বালা।’

অন্ধকারে দুটি নয়ন কালো
ক্ষণেক মোরে দেখলে চেয়ে তবে,
সে কহিল, 'এনেছি এই আলো,
দীপালিতে সাজিয়ে দিতে হবে।'
চেয়ে দেখি লক্ষ দীপের সনে
দীপখানি তার জ্বলে অকারণে।

◆ ◆ ◆

On the slope of the desolate river among tall grasses I asked her, "Maiden, where do you go shading your lamp with your mantle? My house is all dark and lonesome—lend me your light!" She raised her dark eyes for a moment and looked at my face through the dusk. "I have come to the river," she said, "to float my lamp on the stream when the daylight wanes in the west." I stood alone among tall grasses and watched the timid flame of her lamp uselessly drifting in the tide.

In the silence of gathering night I asked her, "Maiden, your lights are all lit—then where do you go with your lamp? My house is all dark and lonesome,—lend me your light." She raised her dark eyes on my face and stood for a moment doubtful. "I have come," she said at last, "to dedicate my lamp to the sky." I stood and watched her light uselessly burning in the void.

In the moonless gloom of midnight I asked her, "Maiden, what is your quest holding the lamp near your heart? My house is all dark and lonesome,—lend me your light." She stopped for a minute and thought and gazed at my face in the dark. "I have brought my light," she said, "to join the carnival of lamps." I stood and watched her little lamp uselessly lost among lights.

◆ ◆ ◆

Among the tall grasses on the deserted river bank
I called her and asked,
"Who are you, walking slowly down the path alone
Covering that lamp with your sari-anchol.
In my house the lamps have not been lit
That lamp of yours, set it here, daughter."
For a moment in the light of the cow-dust hour
She lifted her black eyes to my face
And said, "I'll set my lamp adrift,
That's why I've come to the bank at day's end."
Standing among the tall grasses, I watched
The lamp float away for no reason.

As the dusk advanced to dark
I called her and asked,
"With all the lamps lit in your house
To whom do you offer this lamp?
In my house the lamps have not been lit
That lamp of yours, set it here, daughter."
Two black eyes rested on my face
For a moment, looking at me absently.
She said, "This lamp of mine I'll offer up to the void
A sky lamp for the spirits above."
I watched in a corner of the empty sky
That lamp burn for no reason.

At midnight in the new-moon dark
I went up to her and asked,
"My dear, whom do you seek
Holding the lamp close to your heart?
In my house the lamps have not been lit
That lamp of yours, set it here, daughter."

In the dark two black eyes
    Looked at me a moment, and then
She said, "I've brought this light,
    I must set it among the festival of lamps."
        I watched, amidst a hundred thousand lamps,
            That lamp of hers burn for no reason.

৬৫ 65

হে মোর দেবতা, ভরিয়া এ দেহ প্রাণ
কী অমৃত তুমি চাহ করিবারে পান।
আমার নয়নে তোমার বিশ্বছবি
দেখিয়া লইতে সাধ যায় তব কবি,
আমার মুগ্ধ শ্রবণে নীরব রহি
শুনিয়া লইতে চাহ আপনার গান।
হে মোর দেবতা, ভরিয়া এ দেহ প্রাণ
কী অমৃত তুমি চাহ করিবারে পান।

আমার চিত্তে তোমার সৃষ্টিখানি
রচিয়া তুলিছে বিচিত্র এক বাণী।
তারি সাথে প্রভু মিলিয়া তোমার প্রীতি
জাগায়ে তুলিছে আমার সকল গীতি,
আপনারে তুমি দেখিছ মধুর রসে
আমার মাঝারে নিজেরে করিয়া দান।
হে মোর দেবতা, ভরিয়া এ দেহ প্রাণ
কী অমৃত তুমি চাহ করিবারে পান।

◆ ◆ ◆

WHAT divine drink wouldst thou have, my God, from this overflowing cup of my life?

My poet, is it thy delight to see thy creation through my eyes and to stand at the portals of my ears silently to listen to thine own eternal harmony?

Thy world is weaving words in my mind and thy joy is adding music to them. Thou givest thyself to me in love and then feelest thine own entire sweetness in me.

⬩ ⬩ ⬩

Oh, my lord, having filled my body and life's breath
What nectar would you drink from this.
  Would your desire be met, oh poet,
  Seeing your universe through my eyes,
  Do you want to listen to your own melody
    Standing silent at my enchanted ear.
  Oh, my lord, having filled my body and life's breath
  What nectar would you drink from this.

  Your creation within my heart
  Has composed a wondrous voice.
    And with that, lord, your joy blends
    And awakens all my songs,
    You see yourself in sweet delight
      Having given yourself within me.
    Oh, my lord, having filled my body and life's breath
    What nectar would you drink from this.

জীবনে যা চিরদিন
রয়ে গেছে আভাসে
প্রভাতের আলোকে যা
ফোটে নাই প্রকাশে,
জীবনের শেষ দানে
জীবনের শেষ গানে,
হে দেবতা, তাই আজি
দিব তব সকাশে,
প্রভাতের আলোকে যা
ফোটে নাই প্রকাশে।

কথা তারে শেষ করে
পারে নাই বাঁধিতে,
গান তারে সুর দিয়ে
পারে নাই সাধিতে।
কী নিভৃতে চুপে চুপে
মোহন নবীনরূপে
নিখিল নয়ন হতে
ঢাকা ছিল, সখা, সে।
প্রভাতের আলোকে তো
ফোটে নাই প্রকাশে।

ভ্রমেছি তাহারে লয়ে
দেশে দেশে ফিরিয়া,
জীবনে যা ভাঙাগড়া
সবই তারে ঘিরিয়া।
সব ভাবে সব কাজে
আমার সবার মাঝে
শয়নে স্বপনে থেকে
তবু ছিল একা সে।
প্রভাতের আলোকে তো
ফোটে নাই প্রকাশে।

কত দিন কত লোকে
চেয়েছিল উহারে,
বৃথা ফিরে গেছে তারা
বাহিরের দুয়ারে।
আর কেহ বুঝিবে না,
তোমা-সাথে হবে চেনা
সেই আশা লয়ে ছিল
আপনারই আকাশে,
প্রভাতের আলোকে তো
ফোটে নাই প্রকাশে।

◆ ◆ ◆

SHE who ever had remained in the depth of my being, in the twilight of gleams and of glimpses; she who never opened her veils in the morning light, will be my last gift to thee, my God, folded in my final song.

Words have wooed yet failed to win her; persuasion has stretched to her its eager arms in vain.

I have roamed from country to country keeping her in the core of my heart, and around her have risen and fallen the growth and decay of my life.

Over my thoughts and actions, my slumbers and dreams, she reigned yet dwelled alone and apart.

Many a man knocked at my door and asked for her and turned away in despair.

There was none in the world who ever saw her face to face, and she remained in her loneliness waiting for thy recognition.

◆ ◆ ◆

What has remained a shadow, elusive
All my days
What has not bloomed into expression
In dawn's light,
In life's last gift,
In life's last song,
Oh lord, today I give
In your presence
What has not bloomed
In dawn's light.

Words couldn't exhaust it
Or tie it down,
Songs couldn't attain it
By giving it melody.
In what secret silent
Enchanting new form
It was hidden, my friend,
From everyone's eyes.
But it hadn't bloomed
In dawn's light.

I have traveled with it
Wandered land to land,
Everything in my life
Has been broken or built around it.
In all ways in all my works
Amidst everyone who was mine
It was in my sleep and my dreams
Yet it was alone
But hadn't bloomed
In dawn's light.

On how many days, how many people
Asked for it,
They went back with nothing
From the outer door.
No one else would understand,
Only you would recognize it
It remained with that hope
In its own sky,
But hadn't bloomed
In dawn's light.

৬৭ 67

একাধারে তুমিই আকাশ, তুমি নীড়।
হে সুন্দর, নীড়ে তব প্রেম সুনিবিড়
প্রতি ক্ষণে নানা বর্ণে নানা গন্ধে গীতে
মুগ্ধ প্রাণ বেষ্টন করেছে চারি ভিতে।
সেথা উষা ডান হাতে ধরি স্বর্ণথালা
নিয়ে আসে একখানি মাধুর্যের মালা
নীরবে পরায়ে দিতে ধরার ললাটে;
সন্ধ্যা আসে নম্রমুখে ধেনুশূন্য মাঠে
চিহ্নহীন পথ দিয়ে লয়ে স্বর্ণঝারি
পশ্চিমসমুদ্র হতে ভরি শান্তিবারি।

তুমি যেথা আমাদের আত্মার আকাশ,
অপার সঞ্চারক্ষেত্র, সেথা শুভ্র ভাস;
দিন নাই, রাত্রি নাই, নাই জনপ্রাণী,
বর্ণ নাই, গন্ধ নাই– নাই নাই বাণী।

• • •

THOU art the sky and thou art the nest as well.

O thou beautiful, there in the nest it is thy love that encloses the soul with colours and sounds and odours.

There comes the morning with the golden basket in her right hand bearing the wreath of beauty, silently to crown the earth.

And there comes the evening over the lonely meadows deserted by herds, through trackless paths, carrying cool draughts of peace in her golden pitcher from the western ocean of rest.

But there, where spreads the infinite sky for the soul to take her flight in, reigns the stainless white radiance. There is no day nor night, nor form nor colour, and never, never a word.

◆ ◆ ◆

You yourself are the sky, and you are also the nest.
Oh beautiful, in the nest your deep love
Encloses my enchanted heart every moment on every side
In many colors and many fragrances and songs.
There the dawn with a plate of gold in her right hand
Comes bearing a garland of beauty
To place in silence upon the earth's brow;
Gentle-faced evening comes on unseen paths upon the field
After the cows are gone, bringing in its golden pitcher
The waters of peace from the western ocean.

Where you are the sky of our souls,
Boundless space for transition, there is pure radiance,
There's no day, no night, not creature or life,
There's no color, no fragrance—and there's not,
there is not a word.

তব রবিকর আসে কর বাড়াইয়া
এ আমার ধরণীতে।
সারাদিন দ্বারে রহে কেন দাঁড়াইয়া
কী আছে কী চায় নিতে।
রাতের আঁধারে ফিরে যায় যবে, জানি
নিয়ে যায় বহি মেঘ-আবরণখানি,
নয়নের জলে রচিত ব্যাকুল বাণী
খচিত ললিত গীতে।

নব নব রূপে বরনে বরনে ভরি
বুকে লহ তুলি সেই মেঘ-উত্তরী।
লঘু সে চপল কোমল শ্যামল কালো,
হে নিরঞ্জন, তাই বাস তারে ভালো,
তারে দিয়ে তুমি ঢাক আপনার আলো
সকরুণ ছায়াটিতে।

• • •

THY sunbeam comes upon this earth of mine with arms outstretched and stands at my door the livelong day to carry back to thy feet clouds made of my tears and sighs and songs.

With fond delight thou wrappest about thy starry breast that mantle of misty cloud, turning it into numberless shapes and folds and colouring it with hues everchanging.

It is so light and so fleeting, tender and tearful and dark, that is why thou lovest it, O thou spotless and serene. And that is why it may cover thy awful white light with its pathetic shadows.

◆ ◆ ◆

Your sunbeam comes stretching out its hand
        Towards this my earth.
Why does it stand at my door all day
        What is there, what does it want to take.
When it goes back in the dark of night, I know
It carries back a veil of clouds
Anxious words made of tears
        Strung on pleasant song.

You fill it with new, ever new forms and color upon color
And lift it to your breast, that mantle of cloud,
        It's so light and fleeting, tender and blue and dark,
        Oh spotless one, that's why you love it,
        You cover your own light with it
                In compassionate shadow.

৬৯ 69

এ আমার শরীরের শিরায় শিরায়
যে প্রাণ-তরঙ্গমালা রাত্রিদিন ধায়
সেই প্রাণ ছুটিয়াছে বিশ্বদিগ্‌বিজয়ে,
সেই প্রাণ অপরূপ ছন্দে তালে লয়ে
নাচিছে ভুবনে; সেই প্রাণ চুপে চুপে
বসুধার মৃত্তিকার প্রতি রোমকূপে
লক্ষ লক্ষ তৃণে তৃণে সঞ্চারে হরষে,
বিকাশে পল্লবে পুষ্পে— বরষে বরষে
বিশ্বব্যাপী জন্মমৃত্যুসমুদ্রদোলায়
দুলিতেছে অন্তহীন জোয়ার-ভাঁটায়।
করিতেছি অনুভব, সে অনন্ত প্রাণ
অঙ্গে অঙ্গে আমারে করেছে মহীয়ান।

সেই যুগযুগান্তের বিরাট স্পন্দন
আমার নাড়ীতে আজি করিছে নর্তন।

• • •

THE same stream of life that runs through my veins night and day runs through the world and dances in rhythmic measures.

It is the same life that shoots in joy through the dust of the earth in numberless blades of grass and breaks into tumultuous waves of leaves and flowers.

It is the same life that is rocked in the ocean-cradle of birth and of death, in ebb and in flow.

I feel my limbs are made glorious by the touch of this world of life. And my pride is from the life-throb of ages dancing in my blood this moment.

• • •

These endless waves of life that flow
Night and day in every vein of my body
That life runs through, conquers the universe
That life in wondrous rhythm and beat and meter
Dances in the sky; that life secretly flashes in joy
In a thousand thousand moving blades of grass,
In every pore of the earth's soil,
It blooms in leaf and flower—in every rain and drop
It rocks in the endless ebb and flow
Of the ocean-cradle of birth and death across the universe.
I feel that unending life making me
Glorious in every limb.

That great throb and pulse of age after age
Dances in my veins this day.

৭০ 70

পারবি না কি যোগ দিতে এই ছন্দে রে,
খসে যাবার ভেসে যাবার
ভাঙবারই আনন্দে রে।
পাতিয়া কান শুনিস না যে
দিকে দিকে গগনমাঝে
মরণবীণায় কী সুর বাজে
তপন-তারা-চন্দ্রে রে
জ্বালিয়ে আগুন ধেয়ে ধেয়ে
জ্বলবারই আনন্দে রে।

পাগল-করা গানের তানে
ধায় যে কোথা কেই-বা জানে,
চায় না ফিরে পিছন-পানে
রয় না বাঁধা বন্ধে রে
লুটে যাবার ছুটে যাবার
চলবারই আনন্দে রে।

সেই আনন্দ-চরণপাতে
ছয় ঋতু যে নৃত্যে মাতে,
প্লাবন বহে যায় ধরাতে
বরন গীতে গন্ধে রে
ফেলে দেবার ছেড়ে দেবার
মরবারই আনন্দে রে।

• • •

Is it beyond thee to be glad with the gladness of this rhythm? to be tossed and lost and broken in the whirl of this fearful joy?

All things rush on, they stop not, they look not behind, no power can hold them back, they rush on.

Keeping steps with that restless, rapid music, seasons come dancing and pass away—colours, tunes, and perfumes pour in endless cascades in the abounding joy that scatters and gives up and dies every moment.

◆ ◆ ◆

Won't you be able to join in this rhythm, my dear,
In crumbling away, in floating away,
In the joy of breaking, my dear.
Lay your ear, and don't you hear
Mid-sky and on every side
The melodies that play on death's veena
Amid the sun-moon-stars, my dear,
They light their fires and they rush on
In the joy of burning, my dear.

Who can know where they rush
To the strains of this maddening song,
They don't look towards the rear
Don't stay tied by their ties, my dear,
In losing it all, in running away,
In the joy of moving on, my dear.

In those joyful footfalls
Oh, the six seasons are frenzied in dance,
The floods flow across the earth
In color and song and scent, my dear,
In tossing away, in leaving aside,
In the joy of dying, my dear.

71 ৭১

আমি আমায় করব বড়ো
এই তো আমার মায়া—
তোমার আলো রাঙিয়ে দিয়ে
ফেলব রঙিন ছায়া।
তুমি তোমায় রাখবে দূরে,
ডাকবে তারে নানা সুরে,
আপনারি বিরহ তোমার
আমায় নিল কায়া।

বিরহ-গান উঠল বেজে
বিশ্বগগনময়।
কত রঙের কান্নাহাসি
কতই আশা-ভয়।
কত যে ঢেউ ওঠে পড়ে,
কত স্বপন ভাঙে গড়ে,
আমার মাঝে রচিলে যে
আপন পরাজয়।

এই যে তোমার আড়ালখানি
দিলে তুমি ঢাকা,
দিবানিশির তুলি দিয়ে
হাজার ছবি আঁকা—
এরি মাঝে আপনাকে যে
বাঁধা রেখে বসলে সেজে,
সোজা কিছু রাখলে না, সব
মধুর বাঁকে বাঁকা।

আকাশ জুড়ে আজ লেগেছে
তোমার আমার মেলা।
দূরে কাছে ছড়িয়ে গেছে
তোমার আমার খেলা।

তোমার আমার গুঞ্জরনে
বাতাস মাতে কুঞ্জবনে,
তোমার আমার যাওয়া-আসায়
কাটে সকল বেলা।

• • •

THAT I should make much of myself and turn it on all sides, thus casting coloured shadows on thy radiance—such is thy *maya*.

Thou settest a barrier in thine own being and then callest thy severed self in myriad notes. This thy self-separation has taken body in me.

The poignant song is echoed through all the sky in many-coloured tears and smiles, alarms and hopes; waves rise up and sink again, dreams break and form. In me is thy own defeat of self.

This screen that thou hast raised is painted with innumerable figures with the brush of the night and the day. Behind it thy seat is woven in wondrous mysteries of curves, casting away all barren lines of straightness.

The great pageant of thee and me has overspread the sky. With the tune of thee and me all the air is vibrant, and all ages pass with the hiding and seeking of thee and me.

• • •

That I should make myself great,
That is your illusion, your compassion—
That I should color your light
And cast colored shadows.

Poem 71

You'll keep yourself distant,
And call out with different melodies
To your separation from yourself
        That has found its body in me.

The song of separation rises and resounds
        Through the earth and sky.
Tears and smiles in so many colors
        So much hope and fear.
How many waves rise and fall,
How many dreams break and form,
Oh, you've created in me
        Your defeat of yourself.

This screen with which
        You've hidden yourself,
Is painted with a thousand picures
        With the brush of night and day—
And to all this you've pledged yourself
And sit adorned,
You've left nothing straight or easy; all
        Is curved along such beguiling curves.

Overspreading the sky today
        Is the festival of you and me.
This play of you and me
        Has ranged far and near.
The buzzing of you and me
Maddens the breeze in the dense forest
And all the day passes
        With the coming and going of you and me.

৭২ 72

কে গো অন্তরতর সে।

আমার চেতনা আমার বেদনা
তারি সুগভীর পরশে।
আঁখিতে আমার বুলায় মন্ত্র,
বাজায় হৃদয়বীণার তন্ত্র,
কত আনন্দে জাগায় ছন্দ
কত সুখে দুখে হরষে।
সোনালি রুপালি সবুজে সুনীলে
সে এমন মায়া কেমনে গাঁথিলে,
তারি সে আড়ালে চরণ বাড়ালে
ডুবালে সে সুধাসরসে।
কত দিন আসে কত যুগ যায়
গোপনে গোপনে পরান ভুলায়,
নানা পরিচয়ে নানা নাম লয়ে
নিতি নিতি রস বরষে।

• • •

He it is, the innermost one, who awakens my being with his deep hidden touches.

He it is who puts his enchantment upon these eyes and joyfully plays on the chords of my heart in varied cadence of pleasure and pain.

He it is who weaves the web of this *maya* in evanescent hues of gold and silver, blue and green, and lets peep out through the folds his feet, at whose touch I forget myself.

Days come and ages pass, and it is ever he who moves my heart in many a name, in many a guise, in many a rapture of joy and of sorrow.

◆ ◆ ◆

        Oh, who is he, that innermost one.
My wakening, my pain
        In the depth of his touch.
Touches my eyes with his magic words,
Plays the strings of my heart-veena,
Awakens the rhythm of so many joys
        In so many pleasures sorrows delights.
How he weaves his magic world
Of gold and silver and greens and such deep blues
And from behind these he advances his foot,
        Drowns me in his moonlight-lake.
How many days come how many ages pass
In secret, in secret, enchanting my life
In many guises, taking many names
        Raining down pleasure always, always.

৭৩ 73

বৈরাগ্যসাধনে মুক্তি, সে আমার নয়।

অসংখ্যবন্ধন-মাঝে মহানন্দময়
লভিব মুক্তির স্বাদ। এই বসুধার
মৃত্তিকার পাত্রখানি ভরি বারম্বার
তোমার অমৃত ঢালি দিবে অবিরত
নানাবর্ণগন্ধময়। প্রদীপের মতো
সমস্ত সংসার মোর লক্ষ বর্তিকায়
জ্বালায়ে তুলিবে আলো তোমারি শিখায়
তোমার মন্দির-মাঝে।

ইন্দ্রিয়ের দ্বার
রুদ্ধ করি যোগাসন, সে নহে আমার।
যে-কিছু আনন্দ আছে দৃশ্যে গন্ধে গানে
তোমার আনন্দ রবে তার মাঝখানে।

মোহ মোর মুক্তিরূপে উঠিবে জ্বলিয়া,
প্রেম মোর ভক্তিরূপে রহিবে ফলিয়া।

• • •

Deliverance is not for me in renunciation. I feel the embrace of freedom in a thousand bonds of delight.

Thou ever pourest for me the fresh draught of thy wine of various colours and fragrance, filling this earthen vessel to the brim.

My world will light its hundred different lamps with thy flame and place them before the altar of thy temple.

No, I will never shut the doors of my senses. The delights of sight and hearing and touch will bear thy delight.

Yes, all my illusions will burn into illumination of joy, and all my desires ripen into fruits of love.

◆ ◆ ◆

Freedom through renunciation and austerities,
that's not for me.

Among countless bonds of supreme joy
I'll attain the taste of freedom. You'll pour
Your nectar of many colors and fragrances
Endlessly, into this vessel of the earth's clay
Filling it again and again. Like so many lamps
All my world with its thousand lamp-wicks
Lit at your flame will blaze up
In your temple.

Blocking the doors of my senses
And assuming a yogi's pose, that's not for me.
Whatever joy lies in sight and scent and song
The joy of you will remain at the center of all.

My worldly illusions will burn up as my freedom,
My love will remain and bear fruit as devotion.

আর নাই রে বেলা, নামল ছায়া
ধরণীতে,
এখন চল্ রে ঘাটে কলসখানি
ভরে নিতে।
জলধারার কলস্বরে
সন্ধ্যাগগন আকুল করে,
ওরে, ডাকে আমায় পথের 'পরে
সেই ধ্বনিতে।
চল্ রে ঘাটে কলসখানি
ভরে নিতে।

এখন বিজন পথে করে না কেউ
আসা-যাওয়া—
ওরে, প্রেম-নদীতে উঠেছে ঢেউ,
উতল হাওয়া।
জানি নে আর ফিরব কিনা,
কার সাথে আজ হবে চিনা,
ঘাটে সেই অজানা বাজায় বীণা
তরণীতে।
চল্ রে ঘাটে কলসখানি
ভরে নিতে।

• • •

THE day is no more, the shadow is upon the earth. It is time that I go to the stream to fill my pitcher.

The evening air is eager with the sad music of the water. Ah, it calls me out into the dusk. In the lonely lane there is no passer by, the wind is up, the ripples are rampant in the river.

I know not if I shall come back home. I know not whom I shall chance to meet. There at the fording in the little boat the unknown man plays upon his lute.

◆ ◆ ◆

The day's gone, the shadows have climbed down
On the earth,
Now let's go to the riverbank
And fill our water-pots.
The sweet murmur of flowing water
Makes the evening sky restless
Oh it calls me out to the path
With that sound.
Oh, let's go to the riverbank
And fill our water-pots.

Now on the deserted path no one
Comes and goes—
Oh, waves have risen up in love's river,
The impatient air.
I don't know if I'll be back or not,
Or whom I'll meet today,
At the bank the unknown one plays his veena
In a little boat.
Oh, let's go to the riverbank
And fill our water-pots.

৭৫ 75

মর্তবাসীদের তুমি যা দিয়েছ প্রভু,
মর্তের সকল আশা মিটাইয়া তবু
রিক্ত তাহা নাহি হয়। তার সর্বশেষ
আপনি খুঁজিয়া ফিরে তোমারি উদ্দেশ।

নদী ধায় নিত্যকাজে, সর্ব কর্ম সারি
অন্তহীন ধারা তার চরণে তোমারি
নিত্য জলাঞ্জলিরূপে ঝরে অনিবার।
কুসুম আপন গন্ধে সমস্ত সংসার
সম্পূর্ণ করিয়া তবু সম্পূর্ণ না হয়—
তোমারি পূজায় তার শেষ পরিচয়।
সংসারে বঞ্চিত করি তব পূজা নহে।

কবি আপনার গানে যত কথা কহে
নানা জনে লহে তার নানা অর্থ টানি,
তোমা-পানে ধায় তার শেষ অর্থখানি।

• • •

THY gifts to us mortals fulfil all our needs and yet run back to thee undiminished.

The river has its everyday work to do and hastens through fields and hamlets; yet its incessant stream winds towards the washing of thy feet.

The flower sweetens the air with its perfume; yet its last service is to offer itself to thee.

Thy worship does not impoverish the world.

From the words of the poet men take what meanings please them; yet their last meaning points to thee.*

---

* Using the freedom to drop his own lines to produce a more

♦ ♦ ♦

What you have given us mortals, Lord,
Meets all us mortals' hopes and yet
It is not empty. It seeks out its end
On its own and turns back to you.

The river hastens on its daily tasks, and when all its work
Is done, its endless flow makes its water-offering
Always at your feet in an unceasing stream.
The flower fulfils the entire world
With its fragrance and yet is not itself fulfilled—
Until its final form as a prayer-offering to you.
Worship of you is not by depriving the world.

Whatever words the poet uses in his song,
Many people draw many meanings from them,
Yet their final meaning runs towards you.

---

polished English version, Rabindranath gives us a much more succinct and effective translation.

৭৬ 76

প্রতিদিন আমি হে জীবনস্বামী
দাঁড়াব তোমারি সম্মুখে।
করি জোড়কর, হে ভুবনেশ্বর,
দাঁড়াব তোমারি সম্মুখে।

তোমার অপার আকাশের তলে
বিজনে বিরলে হে—
নম্র হৃদয়ে নয়নের জলে
দাঁড়াব তোমারি সম্মুখে।

তোমার বিচিত্র এ ভবসংসারে
কর্মপারাবারপারে হে,
নিখিলজগৎজনের মাঝারে
দাঁড়াব তোমারি সম্মুখে।

তোমার এ ভবে মোর কাজ যবে
সমাপন হবে হে,
ওগো রাজরাজ, একাকী নীরবে
দাঁড়াব তোমারি সম্মুখে।

• • •

Day after day, O lord of my life, shall I stand before thee face to face? With folded hands, O lord of all worlds, shall I stand before thee face to face?

Under thy great sky in solitude and silence, with humble heart shall I stand before thee face to face?

In this laborious world of thine, tumultuous with toil and with struggle, among hurrying crowds shall I stand before thee face to face?

And when my work shall be done in this world, O King of kings, alone and speechless shall I stand before thee face to face?

◆ ◆ ◆

Every day, oh lord of life,
I will stand face to face before you.
With joined palms, oh ruler of the universe,
I will stand face to face before you.

Beneath your endless sky
Oh in desolation and solitude—
With soft heart and watery eyes
I will stand face to face before you.

In this many-colored world of yours
Oh on the shore of the sea of toil,
In the midst of all the world's people
I will stand face to face before you.

When my work in this world of yours
Is done, oh,
Oh king of kings, alone and silent
I will stand face to face before you.

দেবতা জেনে দূরে রই দাঁড়ায়ে,
আপন জেনে আদর করি নে।
পিতা বলে প্রণাম করি পায়ে,
বন্ধু বলে দু-হাত ধরি নে।
আপনি তুমি অতি সহজ প্রেমে
আমার হয়ে এলে যেথায় নেমে
সেথায় সুখে বুকের মধ্যে ধরে
সঙ্গী বলে তোমায় বরি নে।

ভাই তুমি যে ভায়ের মাঝে প্রভু,
তাদের পানে তাকাই না যে তবু,
ভাইয়ের সাথে ভাগ ক'রে মোর ধন
তোমার মুঠা কেন ভরি নে।
ছুটে এসে সবার সুখে দুখে
দাঁড়াই নে তো তোমারই সম্মুখে,
সঁপিয়ে প্রাণ ক্লান্তিবিহীন কাজে
প্রাণসাগরে ঝাঁপিয়ে পড়ি নে।

• • •

I KNOW thee as my God and stand apart—I do not know thee as my own and come closer. I know thee as my father and bow before thy feet—I do not grasp thy hand as my friend's.

I stand not where thou comest down and ownest thyself as mine, there to clasp thee to my heart and take thee as my comrade.

Thou art the Brother amongst my brothers, but I heed them not, I divide not my earnings with them, thus sharing my all with thee.

In pleasure and in pain I stand not by the side of men, and thus stand by thee. I shrink to give up my life, and thus do not plunge into the great waters of life.

• • •

Knowing you to be God, I stand far away,
I don't embrace you as my own.
I touch your feet as my father's,
I don't take both your hands as a friend.
Where you come down yourself
As mine, with such familiar love,
I don't welcome you warmly, hold you
Happily in my heart as my companion.

You're a brother among brothers, lord,
But still I don't glance at them,
And if I shared my wealth with them
Wouldn't I fill your hand too.
I don't run to stand with everyone
In joy and sorrow, and thus stand with you,
Having given my life to tireless work
I don't leap into the ocean of life.

৭৮ 78

বিধি যেদিন ক্ষান্ত দিলেন
সৃষ্টি করার কাজে
সকল তারা উঠল ফুটে
নীল আকাশের মাঝে।
নবীন সৃষ্টি সামনে রেখে
সুরসভার তলে
ছায়াপথে দেবতা সবাই
বসেন দলে দলে।
গাহেন তাঁরা, 'কী আনন্দ!
এ কী পূর্ণ ছবি!
এ কী মন্ত্র, এ কী ছন্দ,
গ্রহ চন্দ্র রবি!'

হেনকালে সভায় কে গো
হঠাৎ বলি উঠে,
'জ্যোতির মালায় একটি তারা
কোথায় গেছে টুটে!'
ছিঁড়ে গেল বীণার তন্ত্রী,
থেমে গেল গান,
হারা তারা কোথায় গেল
পড়িল সন্ধান।
সবাই বলে, 'সেই তারাতেই
স্বর্গ হত আলো—
সেই তারাটাই সবার বড়ো,
সবার চেয়ে ভালো!'

সেদিন হতে জগৎ আছে
সেই তারাটির খোঁজে—
তৃপ্তি নাহি দিনে, রাত্রে
চক্ষু নাহি বোজে।
সবাই বলে, 'সকল চেয়ে
তারেই পাওয়া চাই।'

সবাই বলে, 'সে গিয়েছে,
ভুবন কানা তাই!'
শুধু গভীর রাত্রিবেলায়
স্তব্ধ তারার দলে—
'মিথ্যা খোঁজা, সবাই আছে'
নীরব হেসে বলে।

◆ ◆ ◆

WHEN the creation was new and all the stars shone in their first splendour, the gods held their assembly in the sky and sang "Oh, the picture of perfection! the joy unalloyed!"

But one cried of a sudden—"It seems that somewhere there is a break in the chain of light and one of the stars has been lost."

The golden string of their harp snapped, their song stopped, and they cried in dismay—"Yes, that lost star was the best, she was the glory of all heavens!"

From that day the search is unceasing for her, and the cry goes on from one to the other that in her the world has lost its one joy!

Only in the deepest silence of night the stars smile and whisper among themselves—"Vain is this seeking! Unbroken perfection is over all!"

◆ ◆ ◆

When the Lord was done
With the work of creation
All the stars burst forth
Amidst the blue sky.

With the new creation before them
        All the deities sit in groups
In the hall of the gods
        Along the Milky Way.
They sing, "What a delight!
        How complete this picture!
What a design, how well fashioned,
        Planets and moon and sun!"

Sometime in the gathering
        Someone suddenly speaks up,
"That garland of radiance
        Has a star torn from it!"
The vina-string was broken,
        The song was stopped,
As everyone set out to find
        Where the lost star had gone.
Everyone says, "It was that very star
        That gave heaven its light—
That very star was biggest of all,
        The best of all!"

Since that day the world
        Has sought that star—
There's no content during the day,
        No eyes close at night.
Everyone says, "Of all the stars
        That's the one we have to find."
Everyone says, "It's because that one's gone,
        That's why the sky is blind!"
Only in the depth of night
        In the motionless group of stars—
Silently they smile and say,
        "This search is in vain, all are here."

যদি তোমার দেখা না পাই প্রভু,
এবার এ জীবনে
তবে তোমায় আমি পাই নি যেন
সে কথা রয় মনে।
যেন ভুলে না যাই, বেদনা পাই
শয়নে স্বপনে।

এ সংসারের হাটে
আমার যতই দিবস কাটে,
আমার যতই দু হাত ভরে ওঠে ধনে,
তবু কিছুই আমি পাই নি যেন
সে কথা রয় মনে।
যেন ভুলে না যাই, বেদনা পাই
শয়নে স্বপনে।

যদি আলসভরে
আমি বসি পথের 'পরে,
যদি ধূলায় শয়ন পাতি সযতনে,
যেন সকল পথই বাকি আছে
সে কথা রয় মনে।
যেন ভুলে না যাই, বেদনা পাই
শয়নে স্বপনে।

যতই উঠে হাসি,
ঘরে যতই বাজে বাঁশি,
ওগো যতই গৃহ সাজাই আয়োজনে,
যেন তোমায় ঘরে হয় নি আনা
সে কথা রয় মনে।
যেন ভুলে না যাই, বেদনা পাই
শয়নে স্বপনে।

◆ ◆ ◆

IF it is not my portion to meet thee in this my life then let me ever feel that I have missed thy sight—let me not forget for a moment, let me carry the pangs of this sorrow in my dreams and in my wakeful hours.

As my days pass in the crowded market of this world and my hands grow full with the daily profits, let me ever feel that I have gained nothing—let me not forget for a moment, let me carry the pangs of this sorrow in my dreams and in my wakeful hours.

When I sit by the roadside, tired and panting, when I spread my bed low in the dust, let me ever feel that the long journey is still before me—let me not forget for a moment, let me carry the pangs of this sorrow in my dreams and in my wakeful hours.

When my rooms have been decked out and the flutes sound and the laughter there is loud, let me ever feel that I have not invited thee to my house—let me not forget for a moment, let me carry the pangs of this sorrow in my dreams and in my wakeful hours.

◆ ◆ ◆

If I don't get to see you, Lord,
This time in this life
Then may it stay in my mind
That I didn't have you.
Let me not forget, let me ache
In my sleep and dreams.

In this world's marketplace
However many days I pass,
However much wealth fills both my hands,
Still may it stay in my mind
That I didn't have anything.
Let me not forget, let me ache
In my sleep and dreams.

If, full of lassitude
I sit beside the road,
If I lay out my bed with care in the dust,
May it stay in my mind
That all the road still remains.
Let me not forget, let me ache
In my sleep and dreams.

However much the laughter rises,
However much the flute plays in the house,
Oh, however much I prepare and decorate,
May it stay in my mind
That I didn't bring you home.
Let me not forget, let me ache
In my sleep and dreams.

আমি শরৎশেষের মেঘের মতো
তোমার গগন-কোণে
সদাই ফিরি অকারণে।
তুমি আমার চিরদিনের
দিনমণি গো—
আজো তোমার কিরণপাতে
মিশিয়ে দিয়ে আলোর সাথে
দেয় নি মোরে বাষ্প ক'রে
তোমার পরশনি।
তোমা হতে পৃথক হয়ে
বৎসর মাস গনি।

ওগো, এমনি তোমার ইচ্ছা যদি,
এমনি খেলা তব,
তবে খেলাও নব নব।
লয়ে আমার তুচ্ছ কণিক
ক্ষণিকতা গো—
সাজাও তারে বর্ণে বর্ণে,
ডুবাও তারে তোমার স্বর্ণে,
বায়ুর স্রোতে ভাসিয়ে তারে
খেলাও যথা-তথা।
শূন্য আমায় নিয়ে রচ
নিত্যবিচিত্রতা।

ওগো, আবার যবে ইচ্ছা হবে
সাঙ্গ কোরো খেলা
ঘোর নিশীথরাত্রিবেলা।
অশ্রুধারে ঝরে যাব
অন্ধকারে গো—
প্রভাতকালে রবে কেবল
নির্মলতা শুভ্রশীতল,

রেখাবিহীন মুক্ত আকাশ
　　হাসবে চারি ধারে।
মেঘের খেলা মিশিয়ে যাবে
　　জ্যোতিসাগরপারে।

◆ ◆ ◆

I AM like a remnant of a cloud of autumn uselessly roaming in the sky, O my sun ever-glorious! Thy touch has not yet melted my vapour, making me one with thy light, and thus I count months and years separated from thee.

If this be thy wish and if this be thy play, then take this fleeting emptiness of mine, paint it with colours, gild it with gold, float it on the wanton wind and spread it in varied wonders.

And again when it shall be thy wish to end this play at night, I shall melt and vanish away in the dark, or it may be in a smile of the white morning, in a coolness of purity transparent.

◆ ◆ ◆

Like a cloud at autumn's end
　　I wander always, aimless,
In a corner of your sky.
Oh you are the sun
　　Of all my days—
Even today
Your falling rays, your touch
Have not made me into vapour,
　　Melted me into light.
I count the years and months
　　Being apart from you.

Oh, if this is what you want,
This is your play,
Then make me play again and anew.
Oh, take this tiny grain
This fleeting me—
Decorate it with color on color,
Dip it in your gold,
Float it on the streaming wind
Play it here and there.
Take my nothingness and make
Wonders every day.

Oh, and then whenever you want
Put an end to this play
In the late dark night.
I'll fall away in a stream of tears
In the darkness, oh—
Only a purity bright and cool
Will remain at dawn,
An unlined, free sky
Will smile all around
And the play of clouds will melt
Into the sea of heavenly light.

৮১ 81

মাঝে মাঝে কতবার ভাবি কর্মহীন
আজ নষ্ট হল বেলা, নষ্ট হল দিন।

নষ্ট হয় নাই, প্রভু, সে-সকল ক্ষণ—
আপনি তাদের তুমি করেছ গ্রহণ
ওগো অন্তর্যামী দেব। অন্তরে অন্তরে
গোপনে প্রচ্ছন্ন রহি কোন্ অবসরে
বীজেরে অঙ্কুররূপে তুলেছ জাগায়ে,
মুকুলে প্রস্ফুটবর্ণে দিয়েছ রাঙায়ে,
ফুলেরে করেছ ফল রসে সুমধুর,
বীজে পরিণত গর্ভ। আমি নিদ্রাতুর
আলস্যশয্যায় 'পরে শ্রান্তিতে মরিয়া
ভেবেছিনু সব কর্ম রহিল পড়িয়া।

প্রভাতে জাগিয়া উঠি মেলিনু নয়ন,
দেখিনু ভরিয়া আছে আমার কানন।

• • •

On many an idle day have I grieved over lost time. But it is never lost, my lord. Thou hast taken every moment of my life in thine own hands.

Hidden in the heart of things thou art nourishing seeds into sprouts, buds into blossoms, and ripening flowers into fruitfulness.

I was tired and sleeping on my idle bed and imagined all work had ceased. In the morning I woke up and found my garden full with wonders of flowers.

• • •

So many times I think again and again, without work
Today the morning is wasted, the day is wasted.

They are not wasted, lord, each of those moments—
Oh, you've taken them yourself, you who know
My innermost thoughts. Inside, deep inside,
Staying hidden, you've found the time
To waken a seed and lift it into a shoot,
You've painted a bud in blooming colors,
Turned flower into fruit sweet with juice,
Made womb into seed. I lay drowsy
On my lazy bed, tired and unmoving,
And thought all my tasks remained undone.

I woke in the morning and opened my eyes
And I saw that my garden was full.

৮২ 82

হে রাজেন্দ্র, তব হাতে কাল অন্তহীন।

গণনা কেহ না করে, রাত্রি আর দিন
আসে যায়, ফুটে ঝরে যুগযুগান্তরা।
বিলম্ব নাহিক তব, নাহি তব ত্বরা—
প্রতীক্ষা করিতে জান। শতবর্ষ ধ'রে
একটি পুষ্পের কলি ফুটাবার তরে
চলে তব ধীর আয়োজন। কাল নাই
আমাদের হাতে; কাড়াকাড়ি করে তাই
সবে মিলে; দেরি কারো নাহি সহে কভু।

আগে তাই সকলের সব সেবা, প্রভু,
শেষ করে দিতে দিতে কেটে যায় কাল—
শূন্য পড়ে থাকে হায় তব পূজা-থাল।

অসময়ে ছুটে আসি, মনে বাসি ভয়—
এসে দেখি, যায় নাই তোমার সময়।

• • •

TIME is endless in thy hands, my lord. There is none to count thy minutes.

Days and nights pass and ages bloom and fade like flowers. Thou knowest how to wait.

Thy centuries follow each other perfecting a small wild flower.

We have no time to lose, and having no time we must scramble for our chances. We are too poor to be late.

And thus it is that time goes by while I give it to every querulous man who claims it, and thine altar is empty of all offerings to the last.

At the end of the day I hasten in fear lest thy gate be shut; but I find that yet there is time.

• • •

Oh lord of this realm, in your hands time is without end.

No one keeps count, nights and days
Come and go, age after age blooms and withers.
Nothing is late for you, you make no haste—
You know how to wait. Through a hundred years
Your calm preparations continue
To make a flower-bud bloom. Time is not
In our hands; and so we all grab and snatch
What we can; we cannot ever bear to delay.

And so in serving everyone who asks, lord,
In finishing that first, the time slips away—
And, ah no, your offering-plate stays bare.

At the wrong time I come running, full of fear—
I come, and I see your time has not yet gone.

৮৩ 83

তোমার সোনার থালায় সাজাব আজ
দুখের অশ্রুধার।
জননী গো, গাঁথব তোমার
গলার মুক্তাহার।
চন্দ্র সূর্য পায়ের কাছে
মালা হয়ে জড়িয়ে আছে,
তোমার বুকে শোভা পাবে আমার
দুখের অলংকার।

ধন ধান্য তোমারি ধন
কী করবে তাও কও।
দিতে চাও তো দিয়ো আমায়,
নিতে চাও তো লও।
দুঃখ আমার ঘরের জিনিস,
খাঁটি রতন তুই তো চিনিস—
তোর প্রসাদ দিয়ে তারে কিনিস,
এ মোর অহংকার।

• • •

MOTHER, I shall weave a chain of pearls for thy neck with my tears of sorrow.

The stars have wrought their anklets of light to deck thy feet, but mine will hang upon thy breast.

Wealth and fame come from thee and it is for thee to give or to withhold them. But this my sorrow is absolutely mine own, and when I bring it to thee as my offering thou rewardest me with thy grace.

• • •

On your golden plate I'll lay out today
A stream of tears of sorrow.
Oh mother, I'll string together
A strand of pearls for your neck.
The moon and sun are wrapped
Around your feet as a garland,
My sorrow will find beauty
As an ornament upon your chest.

Riches and wealth are in your treasury
And you decide what to do with them.
If you want to give, give them to me,
If you want to take, take them.
My sorrow is my household thing,
You can tell if a gem is real—
You could buy it with your grace,
This is my vanity.

৮৪ 84

হেরি অহরহ তোমারি বিরহ
ভুবনে ভুবনে রাজে হে।
কত রূপ ধ'রে কাননে ভূধরে
আকাশে সাগরে সাজে হে।
সারা নিশি ধরি তারায় তারায়
অনিমেষ চোখে নীরবে দাঁড়ায়,
পল্লবদলে শ্রাবণধারায়
তোমারি বিরহ বাজে হে।
ঘরে ঘরে আজি কত বেদনায়
তোমারি গভীর বিরহ ঘনায়,
কত প্রেমে হায় কত বাসনায়
কত সুখে দুখে কাজে হে।
সকল জীবন উদাস করিয়া
কত গানে সুরে গলিয়া ঝরিয়া
তোমারি বিরহ উঠিছে ভরিয়া
আমার হিয়ার মাঝে হে।

• • •

It is the pang of separation that spreads throughout the world and gives birth to shapes innumerable in the infinite sky.

It is this sorrow of separation that gazes in silence all night from star to star and becomes lyric among rustling leaves in rainy darkness of July.

It is this overspreading pain that deepens into loves and desires, into sufferings and joys in human homes; and this it is that ever melts and flows in songs through my poet's heart.

• • •

Oh, always I see it is the want of you
  That pervades the earth and sky.
Oh, how many forms it takes, dressing itself in forest
  And mountain and sky and ocean.
    Through all the night, in star upon star
    It stands silent, with unblinking eyes
    In bunches of new leaves, in late summer's falling rain,
        Oh, the want of you resounds.
It is the deep want of you that thickens today
Into so many aches in every home
Into so much love, oh, so much desire
  Oh, in so many joys and sorrows, so many tasks.
    Making me listless all my life
    Melting and flowing into so many songs and tunes
    Oh, the want of you has filled
        The space within my heart.

প্রভুগৃহ হতে আসিলে যেদিন
বীরের দল
সেদিন কোথায় ছিল যে লুকানো
বিপুল বল।
কোথায় বর্ম, অস্ত্র কোথায়,
ক্ষীণ দরিদ্র অতি অসহায়,
চারি দিক হতে এসেছে আঘাত
অনর্গল,
প্রভুগৃহ হতে আসিলে যেদিন
বীরের দল।

প্রভুগৃহমাঝে ফিরিলে যেদিন
বীরের দল
সেদিন কোথায় লুকাল আবার
বিপুল বল।
ধনুশর অসি কোথা গেল খসি,
শান্তির হাসি উঠিল বিকশি;
চলে গেলে রাখি সারা জীবনের
সকল ফল,
প্রভুগৃহমাঝে ফিরিলে যেদিন
বীরের দল।

• • •

When the warriors came out first from their master's hall, where had they hid their power? Where were their armour and their arms?

They looked poor and helpless, and the arrows were showered upon them on the day they came out from their master's hall.

When the warriors marched back again to their master's hall where did they hide their power?

They had dropped the sword and dropped the bow and the arrow; peace was on their foreheads, and they had left the fruits of their life behind them on the day they marched back again to their master's hall.

◆ ◆ ◆

The day this band of braves came
        Out from their lord's house
Where was their immense power
        Hidden that day.
Where was the armor, where the weapons,
Lean and poor and utterly helpless,
From all four sides the blows came
        Incessant,
The day this band of braves came
        Out from their lord's house.

The day this band of braves went back
        Into their lord's house
Where did they hide their immense power
        Again that day.
Where had the bows and arrows and swords
Been dropped, smiles of peace spread;
They went away leaving the fruits behind
        Of all their lives,
The day this band of braves went back
        Into their lord's house.

৮৬ 86

পাঠাইলে আজি মৃত্যুর দূত
আমার ঘরের দ্বারে,
তব আহ্বান করি সে বহন
পার হয়ে এল পারে।

আজি এ রজনী তিমির-আঁধার,
ভয়ভারাতুর হৃদয় আমার,
তবু দীপ হাতে খুলি দিয়া দ্বার
নমিয়া লইব তারে।
পাঠাইলে আজি মৃত্যুর দূত
আমার ঘরের দ্বারে।

পূজিব তাহারে জোড়-কর করি
ব্যাকুল নয়নজলে,
পূজিব তাহারে পরানের ধন
সঁপিয়া চরণতলে।

আদেশ পালন করিয়া তোমারি
যাবে সে আমার প্রভাত আঁধারি,
শূন্যভবনে বসি তব পায়ে
অর্পিব আপনারে।
পাঠাইলে আজি মৃত্যুর দূত
আমার ঘরের দ্বারে।

• • •

DEATH, thy servant, is at my door. He has crossed the unknown sea and brought thy call to my home.

The night is dark and my heart is fearful—yet I will take up the lamp, open my gates and bow to him my welcome. It is thy messenger who stands at my door.

I will worship him with folded hands, and with tears. I will worship him placing at his feet the treasure of my heart.

He will go back with his errand done, leaving a dark shadow on my morning; and in my desolate home only my forlorn self will remain as my last offering to thee.

• • •

Today you've sent the messenger of death
To the doorstep of my house,
He's carried your summons
And crossed over to come to this side.
Now this night is gloomy and dark,
My heart afflicted with the weight of fear,
Yet I'll open the door, lamp in hand,
And bow and take him in.
Today you've sent the messenger of death
To the doorstep of my house.

I'll worship him with joined palms
And with anxious tears,
Worship him by offering my life's treasures
At his feet.

He'll have carried out your command
And leave, darking my dawn,
And in the empty room, sitting at your feet
I'll offer you me.
Today you've sent the messenger of death
To the doorstep of my house.

আমার ঘরেতে আর নাই সে যে নাই—
যাই আর ফিরে আসি, খুঁজিয়া না পাই।
আমার ঘরেতে নাথ, এইটুকু স্থান—
সেথা হতে যা হারায় মেলে না সন্ধান।
অনন্ত তোমার গৃহ, বিশ্বময় ধাম,
হে নাথ, খুঁজিতে তারে সেথা আসিলাম।
দাঁড়ালেম তব সন্ধ্যা-গগনের তলে,
চাহিলাম তোমা-পানে নয়নের জলে।
কোনো মুখ, কোনো সুখ, আশাতৃষা কোনো
যেথা হতে হারাইতে পারে না কখনো,
সেথায় এনেছি মোর পীড়িত এ হিয়া—
দাও তারে, দাও তারে, দাও ডুবাইয়া।
ঘরে মোর নাহি আর যে অমৃতরস
বিশ্ব-মাঝে পাই সেই হারানো পরশ।

• • •

In desperate hope I go and search for her in all the corners of my room; I find her not.

My house is small and what once has gone from it can never be regained.

But infinite is thy mansion, my Lord, and seeking her I have come to thy door.

I stand under the golden canopy of thine evening sky and I lift my eager eyes to thy face.

I have come to the brink of eternity from which nothing can vanish—no hope, no happiness, no vision of a face seen through tears.

Oh, dip my emptied life into that ocean, plunge it into the deepest fullness. Let me for once feel that lost sweet touch in the allness of the universe.

• • •

She's not in my room any more, she's not—
I go and I come back again, and I cannot find her.
In my room, lord, there is little space—
And what's lost from there cannot be found.
Your home is boundless, your abode spans the universe,
Oh lord, and I have come here to look for her.
I stand beneath your evening sky,
And look at you with tear-filled eyes.
Where no face, no contentment,
No hope or desire is ever lost,
There I have brought this, my wounded heart—
There let it, let it, let it be immersed.
The nectar that is no longer in my room,
Let me find that lost touch amidst the universe.

৪৪

ভাঙা দেউলের দেবতা,
তব বন্দনা রচিতে, ছিন্না
বীণার তন্ত্রী বিরতা।
সন্ধ্যাগগনে ঘোষে না শঙ্খ
তোমার আরতি-বারতা।
তব মন্দির স্থির গম্ভীর,
ভাঙা দেউলের দেবতা!

তব জনহীন ভবনে
থেকে থেকে আসে ব্যাকুল গন্ধ
নববসন্তপবনে।
যে ফুলে রচে নি পূজার অর্ঘ্য,
রাখে নি ও রাঙা চরণে,
সে ফুল ফোটার আসে সমাচার
জনহীন ভাঙা ভবনে।

পূজাহীন তব পূজারি
কোথা সারা দিন ফিরে উদাসীন
কার প্রসাদের ভিখারি।
গোধূলিবেলায় বনের ছায়ায়
চির-উপবাস-ভুখারি
ভাঙা মন্দিরে আসে ফিরে ফিরে
পূজাহীন তব পূজারি।

ভাঙা দেউলের দেবতা,
কত উৎসব হইল নীরব,
কত পূজানিশা বিগতা।
কত বিজয়ায় নবীন প্রতিমা
কত যায় কত কব তা—
শুধু চিরদিন থাকে সেবাহীন
ভাঙা দেউলের দেবতা।

• • •

DEITY of the ruined temple! The broken strings of *Vina* sing no more your praise. The bells in the evening proclaim not your time of worship. The air is still and silent about you.

In your desolate dwelling comes the vagrant spring breeze. It brings the tidings of flowers—the flowers that for your worship are offered no more.

Your worshipper of old wanders ever longing for favour still refused. In the eventide, when fires and shadows mingle with the gloom of dust, he wearily comes back to the ruined temple with hunger in his heart.

Many a festival day comes to you in silence, deity of the ruined temple. Many a night of worship goes away with lamp unlit.

Many new images are built by masters of cunning art and carried to the holy stream of oblivion when their time is come.

Only the deity of the ruined temple remains unworshipped in deathless neglect.

• • •

God of the broken temple,
The broken strings of the veena
    Have ceased making songs praising you.
The conch-shell no longer proclaims
    Your worship across the evening sky.
Your shrine is still and solemn,
    God of the broken temple.

Into your deserted hall
Sometimes a restless fragrance comes
On the new spring air.
The flowers that weren't in your prayer offerings,
Haven't been placed at your painted feet,
The news of those flowers' blooming
Comes into this deserted, broken hall.

Where does he wander all day,
Your worshipper with no offerings,
A beggar at whose palace!
In the cow-dust hour, in forest shadows
He returns wandering to the broken temple
This fasting mendicant, ever hungry
Your worshipper with no offerings.

God of the broken temple,
How many festivals have remained silent,
How many nights of worship have passed.
How many new images for how many Bijoyas*
Are created and carried away, I cannot say—
Only always unserved
Is the god of the broken temple.

* "Bijoya" refers here to the final day of the Bengali Durga Puja festival, when the clay image of the goddess Durga is immersed in the sea or river. A new image is created for the next year's festival.

৮৯ — 89

কোলাহল তো বারণ হল
এবার কথা কানে কানে।
এখন হবে প্রাণের আলাপ
কেবলমাত্র গানে গানে।
রাজার পথে লোক ছুটেছে,
বেচাকেনার হাঁক উঠেছে,
আমার ছুটি অবেলাতেই
দিনদুপুরের মধ্যখানে,
কাজের মাঝে ডাক পড়েছে
কেন যে তা কেই বা জানে।

মোর কাননে অকালে ফুল
উঠুক তবে মুঞ্জরিয়া।
মধ্যদিনে মৌমাছিরা
বেড়াক মৃদু গুঞ্জরিয়া।
মন্দ-ভালোর দ্বন্দ্বে খেটে
গেছে তো দিন অনেক কেটে,
অলস-বেলার খেলার সাথি
এবার আমার হৃদয় টানে।
বিনা-কাজের ডাক পড়েছে
কেন যে তা কেই বা জানে।

• • •

No more noisy, loud words from me—such is my master's will. Henceforth I deal in whispers. The speech of my heart will be carried on in murmurings of a song.

Men hasten to the King's market. All the buyers and sellers are there. But I have my untimely leave in the middle of the day, in the thick of work.

Let then the flowers come out in my garden, though it is not their time; and let the midday bees strike up their lazy hum.

Full many an hour have I spent in the strife of the good and the evil, but now it is the pleasure of my playmate of the empty days to draw my heart on to him; and I know not why is this sudden call to what useless inconsequence!

◆ ◆ ◆

So shouting and noise are forbidden
Now, words only go ear by ear.
Now the conversations of the heart
Will only be song by song.
People rush along the king's road,
The clamor rises of buying and selling,
My respite comes at the wrong time
In the middle of the broad afternoon,
I'm called away in the midst of work
But why, no one knows.

Then let the flowers in my garden
Blossom out of turn.
Let the bees meander at midday
With their slow murmurings.
Much of the day has passed
Toiling in the fight of good and evil,
My playmate of the lazy day
Now comes to tug at my heart.
I'm called away to no purpose
But why, no one knows.

মরণ যেদিন দিনের শেষে আসবে তোমার দুয়ারে
সেদিন তুমি কী ধন দিবে উহারে।
ভরা আমার পরানখানি
সম্মুখে তার দিব আনি,
শূন্য বিদায় করব না তো উহারে—
মরণ যেদিন আসবে আমার দুয়ারে।

কত শরৎ-বসন্ত-রাত,
কত সন্ধ্যা, কত প্রভাত
জীবনপাত্রে কত যে রস বরষে;
কতই ফলে কতই ফুলে
হৃদয় আমার ভরি তুলে
দুঃখসুখের আলোছায়ার পরশে।

যা-কিছু মোর সঞ্চিত ধন
এতদিনের সব আয়োজন
চরমদিনে সাজিয়ে দিব উহারে—
মরণ যেদিন আসবে আমার দুয়ারে।

• • •

On the day when death will knock at thy door what wilt thou offer to him?

Oh, I will set before my guest the full vessel of my life—I will never let him go with empty hands.

All the sweet vintage of all my autumn days and summer nights, all the earnings and gleanings of my busy life will I place before him at the close of my days when death will knock at my door.

• • •

Poem 90

The day that death comes to your door at day's end
What wealth will you give him that day.
    I'll bring and place before him
    My brimful life,
        I won't let him leave with empty hands—
        The day that death comes to my door.

        So many autumn and springtime nights,
        So many evenings, so many dawns
    How much nectar rains into my life's bowl;
        How many fruits, how many flowers
        Have filled my heart
    With joy and sorrow, the touch of light and
                                        shadow.

        Whatever wealth I've saved
        All the things I've made ready all these days
    I'll set out for him the final day—
    The day that death comes to my door.

৯১ 91

ওগো আমার এই জীবনের শেষ পরিপূর্ণতা,
মরণ, আমার মরণ, তুমি কও আমারে কথা।
সারা জনম তোমার লাগি
প্রতিদিন যে আছি জাগি,
তোমার তরে বহে বেড়াই
দুঃখসুখের ব্যথা।
মরণ, আমার মরণ, তুমি
কও আমারে কথা।

যা পেয়েছি, যা হয়েছি
যা-কিছু মোর আশা,
না জেনে ধায় তোমার পানে
সকল ভালোবাসা।
মিলন হবে তোমার সাথে,
একটি শুভ দৃষ্টিপাতে,
জীবনবধূ হবে তোমার
নিত্য অনুগতা;
মরণ, আমার মরণ, তুমি
কও আমারে কথা!

বরণমালা গাঁথা আছে
আমার চিত্তমাঝে,
কবে নীরব হাস্যমুখে
আসবে বরের সাজে।
সেদিন আমার রবে না ঘর,
কেই-বা আপন, কেই-বা অপর,
বিজন রাতে পতির সাথে
মিলবে পতিব্রতা।
মরণ, আমার মরণ, তুমি
কও আমারে কথা।

• • •

O THOU the last fulfilment of life, Death, my death, come and whisper to me!

Day after day have I kept watch for thee; for thee have I borne the joys and pangs of life.

All that I am, that I have, that I hope and all my love have ever flowed towards thee in depth of secrecy. One final glance from thine eyes and my life will be ever thine own.

The flowers have been woven and the garland is ready for the bridegroom. After the wedding the bride shall leave her home and meet her lord alone in the solitude of night.

◆ ◆ ◆

Oh, you, the final fulfillment of this my life,
Death, my death, say something to me!
        All my life I've stayed awake
        Every day, just for you,
For you I wander about
        Bearing the pain of sorrow and joy.
Death, my death,
                Say something to me.

All I've gained, all I've become,
                All of my hopes
All of my love runs towards you
                Unknowing.
        There will be union with you,
        And with one nuptial glance*

* Shubho drishti ("auspicious glance"), here rendered as "nuptial glance," refers to the ceremonial moment during a traditional Bengali Hindu wedding when the bride and groom look at each other for the first time in the ceremony.

Your life-bride will be
    Your eternal follower;
Death, my death,
        Say something to me!

The groom's garland is woven and ready
        In my heart,
When will he come, silent and smiling
        In his bridegroom's finery.
    On that day I will have no home
    No one my own, no one a stranger,
In solitude of night the husband's devotee
    Will join with her husband.
Death, my death,
        Say something to me.

৯২ 92

একদিন এই দেখা হয়ে যাবে শেষ,
পড়িবে নয়ন-'পরে অন্তিম নিমেষ।
পরদিনে এইমত পোহাইবে রাত,
জাগ্রত জগৎ-'পরে জাগিবে প্রভাত।
কলরবে চলিবেক সংসারের খেলা,
সুখে দুঃখে ঘরে ঘরে বহি যাবে বেলা।
সে কথা স্মরণ করি নিখিলের পানে
আমি আজি চেয়ে আছি উৎসুক নয়ানে।
যাহা-কিছু হেরি চোখে কিছু তুচ্ছ নয়,
সকলই দুর্লভ ব'লে আজি মনে হয়।
দুর্লভ এ ধরণীর লেশতম স্থান,
দুর্লভ এ জগতের ব্যর্থতম প্রাণ।
যা পাই নি তাও থাক্, যা পেয়েছি তাও,
তুচ্ছ ব'লে যা চাই নি তাই মোরে দাও।

◆ ◆ ◆

I KNOW that the day will come when my sight of this earth shall be lost, and life will take its leave in silence, drawing the last curtain over my eyes.

Yet stars will watch at night, and morning rise as before, and hours heave like sea waves casting up pleasures and pains.

When I think of this end of my moments, the barrier of the moments breaks and I see by the light of death thy world with its careless treasures. Rare is its lowliest seat, rare is its meanest of lives.

Things that I longed for in vain and things that I got—let them pass. Let me but truly possess the things that I ever spurned and overlooked.

◆ ◆ ◆

One day this power of sight will end,
And my eyelids will close over my eyes for the last time.
The next day, the night will end this same way,
And dawn will wake upon the awakened world.
The world's play will go on with its tumult,
In every home the day will pass in pleasure and sorrow.
With this thought, today I gaze
With eager eyes at the entire universe.
Whatever I see, nothing is trivial,
Everything, I think today, is hard to attain.
Rare is this earth's smallest space,
Rare is the world's most useless life.
What I haven't received, let it be, what I have, that too,
What I thought trivial and didn't want, let me have that now.

৯৩ 93

পেয়েছি ছুটি বিদায় দেহো ভাই,
সবারে আমি প্রণাম করে যাই।
ফিরায়ে দিনু দ্বারের চাবি
রাখি না আর ঘরের দাবি,
সবার আজি প্রসাদবাণী চাই,
সবারে আমি প্রণাম করে যাই।

অনেক দিন ছিলাম প্রতিবেশী,
দিয়েছি যত নিয়েছি তার বেশি।
প্রভাত হয়ে এসেছে রাতি,
নিবিয়া গেল কোণের বাতি,
পড়েছে ডাক চলেছি আমি তাই,
সবারে আমি প্রণাম করে যাই।

• • •

I HAVE got my leave. Bid me farewell, my brothers! I bow to you all and take my departure.

Here I give back the keys of my door—and I give up all claims to my house. I only ask for last kind words from you.

We were neighbours for long, but I received more than I could give. Now the day has dawned and the lamp that lit my dark corner is out. A summons has come and I am ready for my journey.

• • •

I am released, bid me farewell, brother,
I bow to everyone as I leave.

I give back the key to my door,
I keep no claim to my home,
Today I ask for your word of grace,
I bow to everyone as I leave.

Many days we were neighbors,
Whatever I gave, much more did I take.
The night has turned to dawn,
The lamp in the corner is out,
The call has come, and so I depart,
I bow to everyone as I leave.

৯৪ 94

এবার তোরা আমার যাবার বেলাতে
সবাই জয়ধ্বনি কর্‌।
ভোরের আকাশ রাঙা হল রে,
আমার পথ হল সুন্দর।
কী নিয়ে বা যাব সেথা
ওগো তোরা ভাবিস নে তা,
শূন্য হাতেই চলব, বহিয়ে
আমার ব্যাকুল অন্তর।

মালা পরে যাব মিলন-বেশে
আমার পথিক-সজ্জা নয়।
বাধা বিপদ আছে মাঝের দেশে,
মনে রাখি নে সেই ভয়।
যাত্রা যখন হবে সারা
উঠবে জ্বলে সন্ধ্যাতারা,
পূরবীতে করুণ বাঁশরি
দ্বারে বাজবে মধুর স্বর।

• • •

At this time of my parting, wish me good luck, my friends! The sky is flushed with the dawn and my path lies beautiful.

Ask not what I have with me to take there. I start on my journey with empty hands and expectant heart.

I shall put on my wedding garland. Mine is not the red-brown dress of the traveller, and though there are dangers on the way I have no fear in my mind.

The evening star will come out when my voyage

is done and the plaintive notes of the twilight melodies be struck up from the King's gateway.

◆ ◆ ◆

Now at the time of my departure
Raise a cheer, you all.
Oh, the sky of dawn is turned to red,
My path become beautiful.
What I should take there with me
Oh, don't think of that, you all,
I'll walk with empty hands, bearing
My eager heart.

I'll wear a garland and my wedding clothes
The traveler's dress is not mine.
There are barriers and perils in the middle lands,
I do not fear those in my mind.
When the journey is done,
The evening star will blaze up high,
A doleful flute will play
A sweet purabi melody at the door.*

* "Purabi" is a classical raag played or sung in the evening.

৯৫ *95*

জীবনের সিংহদ্বারে পশিনু যে ক্ষণে
এ আশ্চর্য সংসারের মহানিকেতনে,
সে ক্ষণ অজ্ঞাত মোর। কোন্ শক্তি মোরে
ফুটাইল এ বিপুল রহস্যের ক্রোড়ে
অর্ধরাত্রে মহারণ্যে মুকুলের মতো।

তবু তো প্রভাতে শির করিয়া উন্নত
যখনি নয়ন মেলি নিরখিনু ধরা
কনককিরণ-গাঁথা নীলাম্বর-পরা,
নিরখিনু সুখে-দুঃখে-খচিত সংসার,
তখনি অজ্ঞাত এই রহস্য অপার
নিমেষেই মনে হল মাতৃবক্ষসম
নিতান্তই পরিচিত, একান্তই মম।

রূপহীন জ্ঞানাতীত ভীষণ শকতি
ধরেছে আমার কাছে জননী-মুরতি।*

জীবন আমার
এত ভালোবাসি বলে হয়েছে প্রত্যয়,
মৃত্যুরে এমনি ভালো বাসিব নিশ্চয়।

স্তন হতে তুলে নিলে কাঁদে শিশু ডরে—
মুহূর্তে আশ্বাস পায় গিয়ে স্তনান্তরে।

◆ ◆ ◆

I WAS not aware of the moment when I first crossed the threshold of this life.

* Here, Rabindranath joins two Bengali poems to form one poem in English translation.

What was the power that made me open out into this vast mystery like a bud in the forest at midnight!

When in the morning I looked upon the light I felt in a moment that I was no stranger in this world, that the inscrutable without name and form had taken me in its arms in the form of my own mother.

Even so, in death the same unknown will appear as ever known to me. And because I love this life, I know I shall love death as well.

The child cries out when from the right breast the mother takes it away, in the very next moment to find in the left one its consolation.

◆ ◆ ◆

The moment I entered through the lion's gate of life
Into the grand mansion of this wondrous world,
That moment is unknown to me. What power
Bloomed me forth in the lap of this vast mystery
Like a blossom at midnight in a great forest.

Even so, when I raise my head at dawn
And spread my eyes to look at the earth
Dressed in blue, pierced with rays of gold,
I look at the world etched with joy and sorrow,
Then this unknown, boundless mystery
Seems in an instant like my mother's bosom
Completely familiar, absolutely my own.

A formless, tremendous power beyond my knowing
Takes on for me the image of my mother.

Poem 95

Because I love
My life so much, I know now
Death I'll certainly love as well.

The infant lifted from one breast cries out in fear—
But at once takes heart when given the other.

যাবার দিনে এই কথাটি
বলে যেন যাই—
যা দেখেছি যা পেয়েছি
তুলনা তার নাই।
এই জ্যোতিঃসমুদ্র-মাঝে
যে শতদল পদ্ম রাজে
তারি মধু পান করেছি
ধন্য আমি তাই—
যাবার দিনে এই কথাটি
জানিয়ে যেন যাই।

বিশ্বরূপের খেলাঘরে
কতই গেলেম খেলে,
অপরূপকে দেখে গেলেম
দুটি নয়ন মেলে।
পরশ যাঁরে যায় না করা
সকল দেহে দিলেন ধরা।
এইখানে শেষ করেন যদি
শেষ করে দিন তাই—
যাবার বেলা এই কথাটি
জানিয়ে যেন যাই।

• • •

WHEN I go from hence let this be my parting word, that what I have seen is unsurpassable.

I have tasted of the hidden honey of this lotus that expands on the ocean of light, and thus am I blessed—let this be my parting word.

In this playhouse of infinite forms I have had my play and here have I caught sight of him that is formless.

Poem 96

My whole body and my limbs have thrilled with his touch who is beyond touch; and if the end comes here, let it come—let this be my parting word.

◆ ◆ ◆

On the day of my departure
Let me say this before I leave—
What I've seen what I've received
Is incomparable.
The lotus of a hundred petals
That graces this ocean of light
I have drunk its honey
And thus I'm blessed—
On the day of my departure, let me
Tell everyone before I leave.

The one who embodies the infinite universe
How I've played in his playhouse,
Spread open both eyes
And seen the beautiful beyond compare.
The one who cannot be touched
Has touched all of me.
If he ends it here
Let him end it thus—
At the hour of my departure, let me
Tell everyone before I leave.

৯৭ 97

আমার খেলা যখন ছিল তোমার সনে
তখন কে তুমি তা কে জানত।
তখন ছিল না ভয়, ছিল না লাজ মনে
জীবন বহে যেত অশান্ত।
তুমি ভোরের বেলা ডাক দিয়েছ কত
যেন আমার আপন সখার মতো,
হেসে তোমার সাথে ফিরেছিলেম ছুটে
সেদিন কত-না বন-বনান্ত।

ওগো, সেদিন তুমি গাইতে যে-সব গান
কোনো অর্থ তাহার কে জানত।
শুধু সঙ্গে তারই গাইত আমার প্রাণ,
সদা নাচত হৃদয় অশান্ত।
হঠাৎ খেলার শেষে আজ কী দেখি ছবি—
স্তব্ধ আকাশ, নীরব শশী রবি,
তোমার চরণপানে নয়ন করি নত
ভুবন দাঁড়িয়ে আছে একান্ত।

◆ ◆ ◆

When my play was with thee I never questioned who thou wert. I knew nor shyness nor fear, my life was boisterous.

In the early morning thou wouldst call me from my sleep like my own comrade and lead me running from glade to glade.

On those days I never cared to know the meaning of songs thou sangest to me. Only my voice took up the tunes, and my heart danced in their cadence.

Now, when the playtime is over, what is this sudden sight that is come upon me? The world with eyes bent upon thy feet stands in awe with all its silent stars.

◆ ◆ ◆

When I used to play with you
Who knew then who you were.
There was no fear, no sense of diffidence
Life flowed on, turbulent.
You called to me on so many dawns
Like my very own companion,
Through how many forests I ran
Laughing that day with you.

Oh, the songs you'd sing those days
Who knew what they meant.
Only my soul would sing with them,
Always my heart danced, turbulent.
Suddenly at play's end, what's this sight I
see today—
Motionless sky, silent moon and sun,
Eyes bent down upon your feet, the universe
Stands utterly still.

৯৮ *98*

হার-মানা হার পরাব তোমার গলে।
দূরে রব কত আপন বলের ছলে।
জানি আমি জানি ভেসে যাবে অভিমান,
নিবিড় ব্যথায় ফাটিয়া পড়িবে প্রাণ,
শূন্য হিয়ার বাঁশিতে বাজিবে গান,
পাষাণ তখন গলিবে নয়নজলে।

শতদল-দল খুলে যাবে থরে থরে
লুকানো রবে না মধু চিরদিনতরে।
আকাশ জুড়িয়া চাহিবে কাহার আঁখি,
ঘরের বাহিরে নীরবে লইবে ডাকি,
কিছুই সেদিন কিছুই রবে না বাকি
পরম মরণ লভিব চরণতলে।

• • •

I WILL deck thee with trophies, garlands of my defeat. It is never in my power to escape unconquered.

I surely know my pride will go to the wall, my life will burst its bonds in exceeding pain, and my empty heart will sob out in music like a hollow reed, and the stone will melt in tears.

I surely know the hundred petals of a lotus will not remain closed for ever and the secret recess of its honey will be bared.

From the blue sky an eye shall gaze upon me and summon me in silence. Nothing will be left for me, nothing whatever, and utter death shall I receive at thy feet.

• • •

I will place around your neck the garland of my defeat.
How distant can I stay with my strength and guile.
        I know, I know my pride will wash away,
        My life will burst with deep tight pain,
        My empty heart's flute will play its tune,
                And stone will then melt in my tears.

The hundred petals of the lotus will open, layer after layer
Its honey will not be hidden forever.
        Whose sky-wide eye will look,
        Call me out of my home into the silence,
        Nothing that day nothing will remain
                I will gain the ultimate death at your feet.

৯৯ 99

আমি হাল ছাড়লে তবে
তুমি হাল ধরবে জানি।
যা হবার আপনি হবে
মিছে এই টানাটানি।
ছেড়ে দে দে গো ছেড়ে,
নীরবে যা তুই হেরে,
যেখানে আছিস বসে
বসে থাক্ ভাগ্য মানি।

আমার এই আলোগুলি
নেবে আর জ্বালিয়ে তুলি,
কেবলই তারি পিছে
তা নিয়েই থাকি ভুলি।
এবার এই আঁধারেতে
রহিলাম আঁচল পেতে,
যখনি খুশি তোমার
নিয়ো সেই আসনখানি।

• • •

When I give up the helm I know that the time has come for thee to take it. What there is to do will be instantly done. Vain is this struggle.

Then take away your hands and silently put up with your defeat, my heart, and think it your good fortune to sit perfectly still where you are placed.

These my lamps are blown out at every little puff of wind, and trying to light them I forget all else again and again.

But I shall be wise this time and wait in the dark, spreading my mat on the floor; and whenever it is thy pleasure, my lord, come silently and take thy seat here.

• • •

When I give up the helm
        You'll take the helm and steer, I know.
What's to happen will happen on its own
        This pulling and pushing is all a lie.
Let it go oh let it go,
Lose the fight in silence,
Wherever you sit
        Stay seated, and believe it's lucky.

These lamps of mine
Go out and I light them again,
And in doing only that
I forget everything else.
        Now in this darkness
        I stay with my cloth spread out,
        Whenever it pleases you
                Take that as your seat.

রূপসাগরে ডুব দিয়েছি
অরূপ রতন আশা করি;
ঘাটে ঘাটে ঘুরব না আর
ভাসিয়ে আমার জীর্ণ তরী।
সময় যেন হয় রে এবার
ঢেউ খাওয়া সব চুকিয়ে দেবার,
সুধায় এবার তলিয়ে গিয়ে
অমর হয়ে রব মরি।

যে গান কানে যায় না শোনা
সে গান যেথায় নিত্য বাজে,
প্রাণের বীণা নিয়ে যাব
সেই অতলের সভামাঝে।
চিরদিনের সুরটি বেঁধে
শেষ গানে তার কান্না কেঁদে,
নীরব যিনি তাঁহার পায়ে
নীরব বীণা দিব ধরি।

◆ ◆ ◆

I DIVE down into the depth of the ocean of forms, hoping to gain the perfect pearl of the formless.

No more sailing from harbour to harbour with this my weather-beaten boat. The days are long passed when my sport was to be tossed on waves.

And now I am eager to die into the deathless.

Into the audience hall by the fathomless abyss where swells up the music of toneless strings I shall take this harp of my life.

I shall tune it to the notes of for ever, and, when it has sobbed out its last utterance, lay down my silent harp at the feet of the silent.

• • •

I have dived into the sea of forms
Hoping for the formless gem;
Harbor to harbor I'll wander no more
Floating my worn-out boat.
May it now be time
To end all the rocking on waves,
Now I'll sink into the nectar
And in dying, remain deathless.

The song inaudible to the ear
There that song plays forever,
I'll take the veena of my life
Into the gathering in that bottomless world.
Setting it to eternity's tune
Crying out its tears in a final song,
I'll lay down my silent veena
At the feet of the silent one.

১০১   101

গান দিয়ে যে তোমায় খুঁজি
বাহির মনে
চিরদিবস মোর জীবনে।
নিয়ে গেছে গান আমারে
ঘরে ঘরে দ্বারে দ্বারে,
গান দিয়ে হাত বুলিয়ে বেড়াই
এই ভুবনে।

কত শেখা সেই শেখালো,
কত গোপন পথ দেখালো,
চিনিয়ে দিল কত তারা
হৃদ্‌গগনে।
বিচিত্র সুখদুখের দেশে
রহস্যলোক ঘুরিয়ে শেষে
সন্ধ্যাবেলায় নিয়ে এল
কোন্ ভবনে!

◆ ◆ ◆

EVER in my life have I sought thee with my songs. It was they who led me from door to door, and with them have I felt about me, searching and touching my world.

It was my songs that taught me all the lessons I ever learnt; they showed me secret paths, they brought before my sight many a star on the horizon of my heart.

They guided me all the day long to the mysteries of the country of pleasure and pain, and, at last, to what palace gate have they brought me in the evening at the end of my journey?

◆ ◆ ◆

With my songs it is you I look for
Reaching out
All the days of my life.
My songs have taken me
From house to house, door to door,
With my songs I feel for, touch
This world.

How many teachings they have taught,
How many hidden paths revealed,
How many stars they've shown me
On my heart's heaven.
Around the land of many-colored joys and sorrows,
They lead me, through this mystery-world, and
In the end, at the evening hour, to what palace
Do they bring me!

১০২ 102

তোমায় চিনি বলে আমি করেছি গরব
লোকের মাঝে;
মোর আঁকা পটে দেখেছে তোমায়
অনেকে অনেক সাজে।
কত জনে এসে মোরে ডেকে কয়
'কে গো সে', শুধায় তব পরিচয়—
'কে গো সে।'
তখন কী কই, নাহি আসে বাণী,
আমি শুধু বলি, 'কী জানি! কী জানি!'
তুমি শুনে হাস, তারা দুষে মোরে
কী দোষে।

তোমার অনেক কাহিনী গাহিয়াছি আমি
অনেক গানে।
গোপন বারতা লুকায়ে রাখিতে
পারি নি আপন প্রাণে।
কত জন মোরে ডাকিয়া কয়েছে,
'যা গাহিছ তার অর্থ রয়েছে
কিছু কি।'
তখন কী কই, নাহি আসে বাণী,
আমি শুধু বলি, 'অর্থ কী জানি!'
তারা হেসে যায়, তুমি হাস বসে
মুচুকি।

[তোমায় জানি না চিনি না এ কথা বলো তো
কেমনে বলি।
খনে খনে তুমি উঁকি মারি চাও,
খনে খনে যাও ছলি।
জ্যোৎস্নানিশীথে পূর্ণ শশীতে,
দেখেছি তোমার ঘোমটা খসিতে,
আঁখির পলকে পেয়েছি তোমায়
লখিতে।

বক্ষ সহসা উঠিয়াছে দুলি,
অকারণে আঁখি উঠেছে আকুলি,
বুঝেছি হৃদয়ে ফেলেছ চরণ
চকিতে।

তোমায় খনে খনে আমি বাঁধিতে চেয়েছি
কথার ডোরে।
চিরকাল-তরে গানের সুরেতে
রাখিতে চেয়েছি ধরে।
সোনার ছন্দে পাতিয়াছি ফাঁদ,
বাঁশিতে ভরেছি কোমল নিখাদ,
তবু সংশয় জাগে ধরা তুমি
দিলে কি!
কাজ নাই, তুমি যা খুশি তা করো—
ধরা না'ই দাও মোর মন হরো,
চিনি বা না চিনি প্রাণ উঠে যেন
পুলকি।]

• • •

I BOASTED among men that I had known you. They see your pictures in all works of mine. They come and ask me, "Who is he?" I know not how to answer them. I say, "Indeed, I cannot tell." They blame me and they go away in scorn. And you sit there smiling.

I put my tales of you into lasting songs. The secret gushes out from my heart. They come and ask me, "Tell me all your meanings." I know not how to answer them. I say, "Ah, who knows what they mean!" They smile and go away in utter scorn. And you sit there smiling.*

---

* Rabindranath chooses not to translate the last two stanzas of the original; I have included them in my translation.

◆ ◆ ◆

I have boasted to people
That I know you;
Many have seen you, adorned many ways
On the canvases I have painted.
How many come and call me and say,
"Who is that," asking to know about you—
"Who is that."
What can I say then, words don't come,
I only say, "I can't tell. Really I can't!"
You hear this and smile, and they blame me
For some offense.

I have sung many stories of you
In many songs.
These secret matters I haven't been able
To hide in my heart.
How many people have called to me and said,
"What you sing, is there any meaning
To it at all?"
What can I say then, words don't come,
I only say, "I can't tell what it means!"
They laugh and walk away, you sit there
Smiling quietly.

[If you say I don't know you, don't recognize you,
How can I agree,
From moment to moment you peek at me,
Moment to moment you trick me and vanish.
On late moonlit nights, in the full moon,
I've seen your veil slip, and I've caught
In the blink of an eye
A glimpse of you.

Suddenly there was a trembling in my chest,
For no reason my eyes became eager,
I knew your footstep in my heart.
Instantly.

I've tried to tie you with the cords of words
At every moment.
I've always tried to hold you fast
In the tunes of songs.
I've laid traps in golden verse,
Filled my flute with plaintive notes,
Still my doubts arise, did you
Let yourself be caught!
You have no work, you do what you want—
All right, you won't be caught, you take my
thoughts,
Whether I know you or not, it's as though my heart
Leaps up in delight.]

১০৩ 103

একটি নমস্কারে, প্রভু,
একটি নমস্কারে
সকল দেহ লুটিয়ে পড়ুক
তোমার এ সংসারে।
ঘন শ্রাবণ-মেঘের মতো
রসের ভারে নম্র নত
একটি নমস্কারে, প্রভু,
একটি নমস্কারে
সমস্ত মন পড়িয়া থাক্
তব ভবন-দ্বারে।

নানা সুরের আকুল ধারা
মিলিয়ে দিয়ে আত্মহারা
একটি নমস্কারে, প্রভু,
একটি নমস্কারে
সমস্ত গান সমাপ্ত হোক
নীরব পারাবারে।
হংস যেমন মানসযাত্রী
তেমনি সারা দিবসরাত্রি
একটি নমস্কারে, প্রভু,
একটি নমস্কারে
সমস্ত প্রাণ উড়ে চলুক
মহামরণ পারে।

• • •

IN one salutation to thee, my God, let all my senses spread out and touch this world at thy feet.

Like a rain-cloud of July hung low with its burden of unshed showers let all my mind bend down at thy door in one salutation to thee.

Let all my songs gather together their diverse strains into a single current and flow to a sea of silence in one salutation to thee.

Like a flock of homesick cranes flying night and day back to their mountain nests let all my life take its voyage to its eternal home in one salutation to thee.

◆ ◆ ◆

In bowing to you just once, lord,
    In bowing to you just once
Let all of me sprawl
    On this earth of yours.
Like a heavy monsoon cloud, soft,
Hanging low with the weight of its nectar
    In bowing to you just once, lord,
        In bowing to you just once
    Let all my mind lie here
        At the door to your hall.

The eager streams of different tunes
Blending together to lose themselves
    In bowing to you just once, lord,
        In bowing to you just once
    Let all the songs end
        In the silent ocean.
As the swan returns to its mountain lake*
In the same way, all night and day
    In bowing to you just once, lord,

---

* According to legend, the birthplace of the swan is the Manas Sarovar, a lake created, according to Hindu mythology, by the mind of Lord Brahma and now associated with Lake Mansarovar in Tibet.

In bowing to you just once
Let all my life fly on
To death's vast shore.

Translator's Afterword

I HOPE THESE TRANSLATIONS have warranted the paper used in their printing and your time spent reading them. As a brief afterword to this act of translation, I add one final thought for your consideration.

For every translation, the translator must consider, I believe, the greater implications of his or her act of translation. Some years ago, I argued that translating from a formerly (and perhaps still) colonized people's language into the language of the (supposedly former) colonizer is an act laden with historical imbalance and contemporary political weight. Does the translation bring forth the beauty of the colonized literature and therefore add to the colonized people's cultural power, or does it make explicit the superiority of the colonizer's language as that which is necessary for the colonized literature to gain greater currency? (I believe it does both.)

Further complicating this already fraught act is the secondary question of who does the translation. The identity of the translator, I have argued* (to much consternation and dispute), is particularly significant, even critical, in the colonized–colonizer setting. For a translation from a formerly colonized people's language, such as Bengali, into the language of the former colonizer, English, it is a significant question whether the translator identifies as a member of the colonizing people or the colonized people.

For a British person translating Tagore, as several have, the act serves to underline the intervention of the British colonizer and

---

* Please see the Introduction to the hardcover edition (or the Introduction and Afterword to the paperback edition) of Prasenjit Gupta (trans.), *Indian Errant: Selected Stories of Nirmal Verma*, New Delhi: Indialog Publications, 2002.

his language and perpetuates the act of colonization, even though in a supposedly postcolonial context. Conversely, if an Indian or Bangladeshi person translates Tagore into English, the act may be interpreted as one of resistance to colonization, in that the translator seeks to demonstrate her possession of the colonizer's language and thus add the heft of her work to that language and that literature, thereby claiming a tiny fraction of that language and that literature—as recompense, perhaps, for the much larger price exacted by the colonizer from the colonized. This is not to say that the question of linguistic power vanishes altogether, but at least the fact of the translator's identity in the second case mitigates the negative political effects of the translation to some degree.

That, then, is my further justification for undertaking this translation: as an act of political resistance to previous translations of Tagore by British translators. Baldly put, it is galling for many Indian readers to see a British translator's name on a work of Indian literature. More and more excellent Indian translators are overtaking their British predecessors, and I celebrate the victories I see in their work. I hope my translation of this collection too will overwrite in some small way the names of British translators on this Indian masterpiece.

The Perpetual-Motion Machine That Is Colonialism

As I hope I've indicated above, every act of translation of an Indian work by a British translator is an act that perpetuates colonialism.

This is how the whole business of colonialism works in the context of translation. First the colonizers enter our country under the guise of trade and commerce, and then, with money and gunpowder and a good measure of chicanery, they take control of large chunks of the country and drain it of wealth and dignity. Then some of them turn their attention to our literature and culture, and they start putting their names on our creations.

For example: Gitanjali by Rabindranath Tagore, translated into English by George Horseduke. Never mind that the aforesaid Tagore did an excellent translation himself. Colonial arrogance knows no bounds. This is what they're still doing.

An unbiased observer, if you could find one, would see the fiendish cunning of this. What the colonizers say is they're honoring a great Indian writer by making his works accessible to a larger audience, to an English-speaking audience, and thus doing him and Indian literature a great service. But what they're also doing is adding their name to this great Indian writer's work, stamping its title page with their British lineage, and claiming it as one of their own. A masterful move! A gleaming double-edged sword, ideal for postcolonial exploitation.

For living Indian writers who are honored in this fashion, the choice is especially difficult. Who doesn't want to be recognized internationally, to be translated into English by a native English speaker with such a fine English name as Horseduke? Even the few who realize the imperial motive behind this honor—and, let's face it, not everyone has the percipience to recognize colonial cunning, which over the centuries has evolved into an art—are torn between expanding their own reputation and saving Indian literature from these colonial depredations.

And then—the most polished, most effective reciprocating piston in this monstrous machine—the English translator, the redoubtable Horseduke of impeccable taste and impressive vocabulary, may not himself recognize the imperial grasp of his translation project. He believes he is doing a good thing. That allows him to be sincere in his dealings with the Indian writer, whom he genuinely admires.

You have to be impressed by the diabolical cleverness of this whole scheme. Even the agent of this duplicitous literary conquest isn't aware of his duplicity. He's a naïve missionary, blithely spreading enlightenment and salvation. (But you know that in the missionary position, only one thing can happen.)

Finally and most efficiently, no one is needed to run the scheme! Once all the parts have been put in place—the predatory colonization, the draining of resources, the dependence on Britain for self-esteem, etc.—the machine can function on its own, stamping Indian literature with English names, churning out great works of now-English literature, with even the central participants proudly unaware of what they're doing. That's the tragic beauty of this ultimate perpetual-motion colonizing machine.

Index of First Lines (Bengali)

Index of First Words (Tagore Translations)

Index of First Words (Tagore Translations)

Index of First Words (Tagore Translations)

Index of First Words (Tagore Translations)

Index of First Lines (Gupta Translations)

Index of First Lines (Gupta Translations)

Index of First Lines (Gupta Translations)

About the Author

Rabindranath Tagore (1861–1941) is the greatest Indian poet of the last few centuries and perhaps of all time. Also philosopher, educator, playwright, musician, novelist, and painter, "Gurudeb" lives on in the hearts and homes of his native Bengal and of Bengalis across the world.

About the Translator

Prasenjit Gupta's previous books of translation include *Indian Errant,* a collection of short stories by Nirmal Verma translated from Hindi, and *Matchbox*, a collection of short stories by Ashapurna Debi translated from Bengali. Other translations appear on the web site PARABAAS.com. Gupta's other works include *A Brown Man and Other Stories* and the children's comic adventure book *To the Blue King's Castle* as well as other novels written under a pen-name. Gupta holds an MFA in Fiction from the Iowa Writers' Workshop and a Ph.D. in Comparative Literature focusing on Translation Studies. He has won a Fulbright award for his translations of Nirmal Verma's fiction and a U.S. National Endowment for the Arts fellowship for his translations of Ashapurna Debi's fiction.

Other PARABAAS Titles in English

Bibhutibhushan Bandyopadhyay, *Distant Thunder*
Translated by Chhanda Chattopadhyay Bewtra, 2018

Samarendra Narayan Roy, *Memories of Madhupur: Mid-Century Vignettes from East of India*, 2018

The Scent of Sunlight: Poems by Jibanananda Das
Translated by Clinton B. Seely, 2019

Nabaneeta Dev Sen, *Looking for an Address*
Translated by Chhanda Chattopadhyay Bewtra, 2020

Buddhadeva Bose, *The Land Where I Found It All*
Translated by Nandini Gupta, 2021

Bibhutibhushan Bandyopadhyay, *Ichhamoti*
Translated by Chhanda Chattopadhyay Bewtra, 2023

Cautionary Tales: Short Stories by Rabindranath Tagore
Translated by Carolyn B. Brown, 2025

Binoy Majumdar, *Hospital Poems of Mathematics and Madness*
Translated by Arunava Sinha, 2025

Deben Roy, *Brown Man in White Light,* 2025

www.ingramcontent.com/pod-product-compliance
Lightning Source LLC
LaVergne TN
LVHW091520200926
848483LV00002B/261

* 9 7 8 1 9 4 6 5 8 2 4 0 9 *